JOHN GREENLEAF WHITTIER
As a Young Man

The POEMS *of* JOHN GREENLEAF WHITTIER

*Fifty-four of His Poems
with Notes and
Biographical Sketch*

WHITTIER HOMESTEAD
EDITION

HAVERHILL,
MASSACHUSETTS

**Copyright 1945 & 1983
Wilbert F. Barrett, Esq. &
Trustees of the Whittier Homestead**

All Rights Reserved

**Third Printing, 1995
Printed in the United States of America**

This book was originally compiled and privately published in 1945 by Haverhill Attorney Wilbert F. Barrett. It was first reprinted in 1983 by the Whittier Homestead Trustees and for this second time by the HPL PRESS.

**Published for the Whittier Homestead Trustees
by
HPL PRESS of the Haverhill Public Library
99 Main Street; Haverhill, Massachusetts 01830-5092**

ISBN: 1-878651-04-8

Foreword

In recent years the poetry of John Greenleaf Whittier has come to be recognized at its true value. Although known as the "poet laureate of abolition," Whittier's masterpiece is "Snow Bound," acknowledged to be the greatest poem of its type written during the nineteenth century, his "Barbara Frietchie" is the most stirring and the best of modern ballads and his "At Last" is claimed by many authorities to be the finest devotional poem written by an American and one of the best ever written outside of the Book of Psalms.

Our Government has recognized Whittier's achievements by issuing a postage stamp in his honor, thereby placing him among the five greatest poets of our Country. This volume of fifty-four selected poems is offered in the hope that many may understand, enjoy and appreciate the value of his poetry.

Appreciation for the assistance of Donald K. Campbell, librarian of the Haverhill Public Library, in the preparation of this volume is hereby acknowledged.

THE PUBLISHER.

EARLY LIFE

John Greenleaf Whittier was born in the family homestead on Whittier Road (off Route 110) in Haverhill, Mass., on December 17, 1807, the second child of John and Abigail Hussey Whittier. His father, John Whittier, had been born in the same family homestead in 1760 and he had married Abigail Hussey in 1804 when he was forty-four years of age and she only twenty-one. The other three children in the Whittier family consisted of Mary, born in 1806; Matthew Franklin, born in 1812, and Elizabeth, born in 1815.

The homestead was built in 1688 by Thomas B. Whittier, born in England in 1620, who came to America in 1638, moving to Haverhill in 1647, seven years after its settlement. Thomas married Ruth Green by whom he had ten children, one of whom was Joseph B. Whittier, born in 1669 and married to Mary Peasley in 1694. Upon the death of his father, Joseph bought out the interests of the other heirs in the homestead. Joseph and Mary Whittier had nine children of whom their son Joseph, born in 1716 in the homestead, was the grandfather of the poet. He married Sarah Greenleaf in 1739. They had eleven children of whom John was the poet's father, and from his grandmother, Sarah Greenleaf, the poet obtained his middle name. John Whittier and his brother Moses bought out the interests of the other heirs of their father, Joseph, in the homestead for $1700.00. They operated the farm together until Moses died in 1824. Thereafter, John operated the farm until his death in 1830.

Of the children born to John and Abigail Whittier, Mary married Joseph Caldwell, and they later lived in Newburyport where John Greenleaf Whittier often visited during the last years of his life. Matthew Franklin Whittier became a custom house employee in Boston and held this position until his death in 1883. His daughter, Elizabeth, kept house for her uncle, after the death of Greenleaf's sister Elizabeth on September 3, 1864.

The poet was named John for his father and Greenleaf for his grandmother's family. He was called "Greenleaf" by the members of his family to distinguish him from his father. A sufferer from heart trouble from early manhood,

BIOGRAPHICAL SKETCH

Greenleaf never felt certain of sufficient strength to be able to earn enough money to support a wife and family of his own and also his mother, his invalid sister Elizabeth and his aunt Mercy Evans Hussey (mother's sister), who were dependent upon him, and so he was forced to remain single to support the family burdens he inherited.

The first Whittier to become a Quaker was Joseph for he married a Quaker, Mary Peasley, in 1694 and joined that sect. Their son Joseph was a Quaker, and he married a Quaker girl, Sarah Greenleaf. The poet's father was a Quaker and he also married a Quaker, Abigail Hussey.

John Greenleaf was a Quaker all of his life. He wore the long, black Quaker coat and in early life the broad-brimmed Quaker hat, was extremely neat about his person and was clean shaven until over 60 years of age. The familiar picture of the old gentleman with the full beard was made only a few years before his death. Whittier used the Quaker dialect during most of his conversations but, when the occasion required, he would drop the dialect and use direct and forceable language.

EARLY EDUCATION

While a boy on the farm, John Greenleaf Whittier was forced to perform the many chores of the farm boy of that day, which meant that he worked from sun-up until long after sun-down. His early schooling was limited to the East Parish School in Haverhill. At the age of nineteen he entered the Haverhill Academy, a private school with a high school standing, which was organized and where classes started on May 1, 1827. Whittier was a student during the first term of thirteen weeks and also for the term that began on May 1 the following year.

Opening exercises of the Haverhill Academy were held on April 30, 1827, in its building, which still stands on Winter Street, in Haverhill, and is now used by the Superintendent of Schools for his offices. Whittier wrote an "ode" for the occasion that was printed in the program but it did not carry his name for credit. Charges for the thirteen weeks tuition were $4.00 plus $2.00 for the French courses, so that the total cost of the tuition for Whittier's two terms at the "Academy" was $12.00. Yet he became an overseer of Harvard University in 1858, received from it in 1860 the honorary degree of master of arts, was elected a trustee of Brown University in 1869, and received the degree of doctor of laws from Harvard in 1886.

To pay for his first term tuition, Whittier worked during the winter of 1826-27 making slippers for eight cents a pair that retailed for twenty-five cents. To pay for the second term tuition, Whittier taught school during the winter of 1827-28 at the Birch Meadow School in West Amesbury, now Merrimac, and by keeping books for a Haverhill merchant during the spring of 1828.

WORKING

After finishing his second term at the Academy, Whittier was unable to go to college for lack of funds. It was therefore necessary for him to seek employment. While a student at the Academy, he had boarded in the family of Abijah W. Thayer, the editor of the Haverhill Gazette, and during the 1828 term had collected much of the material for the B. L. Mirick's History of Haverhill that was published by Thayer in 1832. At this time, Whittier had something of a local reputation as a writer and poet for his first published poem, "The Exile's Departure," had been published by William Lloyd Garrison in the Newburyport Free Press on June 8, 1826, and he had since then written scores of poems and some prose that had been published in many New England newspapers and magazines.

In January 1829, Whittier secured work as an editor for the American Manufacturer, a pro-Clay weekly that advocated a protective tariff, was anti-slavery and anti-Harrison, who was then seeking re-election to the presidency. Whittier held this position that paid him $9.00 a week for about eight months and then returned to the farm, as his father's health was failing and he was needed to help harvest the crops. Whittier worked as editor of the Essex Gazette during the winter of 1830.

After his father's death in June 1830, Whittier secured work as editor of the New England Weekly Review at Hartford, Conn., as its owner and editor, George Prentice, had accepted the position of one of Henry Clay's campaign managers in his fight for the presidency against Andrew

BIOGRAPHICAL SKETCH

Jackson. The following March (1831) Whittier suffered such a severe nervous breakdown from over-work that his heart was affected to such an extent that he was unable thereafter to take a position that required long hours of laborious mental effort. He was therefore forced to rest at his Haverhill home until August, 1831, when he returned to his job on the Weekly Review, but in December of the same year he suffered another attack that caused him again to return home to rest. He was forced to relinquish this position as too much for his strength. During 1832, Whittier remained about the farm and, when able, in the following winter, did some editorial work for the Haverhill Gazette.

ANTI-SLAVERY

In 1830, slavery was the most important political issue before the country. John Greenleaf Whittier was a bitter foe of slavery. In 1833 he wrote and published at his own expense "Justice and Expediency" in which he demanded the immediate abolition of slavery and attacked the Colonization Society for its failure to act because of its officers playing politics. As a result of this publication, Whittier was placed in the fore-front as one of the nation's anti-slavery leaders. On December 4, 1833, he was a delegate to the National Anti-Slavery Convention at Philadelphia, his expenses being paid by Samuel E. Sewall, a Boston lawyer. One-third of the delegates to the convention were Quakers. Whittier was the youngest delegate and William Lloyd Garrison the most noted. Garrison was the chairman of the committee, and Whittier was a member, to draft the Declaration of Sentiments which was accepted by the convention on December 6, 1833.

On April 3, 1834, a local branch of the Anti-Slavery Society was formed in Haverhill with John Greenleaf Whittier its corresponding secretary. At this time, Whittier was one of the paid secretaries of the Anti-Slavery Society and acted as a publicist for it. A branch of the Female Anti-Slavery Society was also formed in which Elizabeth Whittier took an active part. In 1835, a mob broke up their anti-slavery meeting in Haverhill and attempted to hang the speakers.

On September 20, 1834, William Lloyd Garrison published in the Liberator, Whittier's poem entitled "Stanzas," which has also been known as "Follen" and "Expostulation." It had an immediate, nation-wide circulation. The poem is based on the Act of Parliament in 1833 freeing all of the 800,000 slaves in the British Dominions, while the United States still held in slavery over 2,500,000.

In 1835, Whittier was elected a Representative to the General Court of Massachusetts. His work as a legislator was noted for his advocacy of the abolition of capital punishment. It was during this year that he wrote "The Yankee Girl" and "The Prisoner for Debt."

On September 4, 1835, Whittier accompanied the English abolition advocate, George Thompson, to Concord, N. H., where they were attacked by a pro-slavery mob, pelted with rocks and eggs, forced to hide until early the next morning, when they were able to make their escape by fast driving through the crowd, with Whittier disguised, by the exchange of his broad-brimmed Quaker hat, as a clergyman.

In the summer of 1837, Whittier was attending the Essex County Anti-Slavery Convention at the estate of Charles Butler in Newburyport, as no hall or church was available for the meeting, when it was broken up by a pro-slavery mob and Whittier had to leave the convention on the run.

On May 7, 1836, Whittier became editor of the Essex Gazette, then owned by Erastus Brooks, and when Brooks sold this newspaper on June 2, 1836, to Whittier's brother-in-law, Jacob Caldwell, Whittier was made managing editor. The new managing editor then changed the policy of the newspaper to that of a radical anti-slavery sheet with the result that the income from both subscriptions and advertising dropped sharply and consequently one-half interest in the newspaper had to be sold to Jeremiah Spofford, of East Bradford (now Groveland) who became the managing editor and Whittier his assistant. On December 17, 1836, Whittier ceased all connection with this newspaper and returned to his home which was then in Amesbury. This was not a serious loss as his eight months earnings totaled only $90.00.

Up until 1836, Whittier made his home at the old homestead in Haverhill but, in that year, he sold the farm to

BIOGRAPHICAL SKETCH

Aaron Chase for $3000 and bought a cottage house on Friend Street, Amesbury, Mass., for $1200.00. This home was close to the Quaker meeting house. Thereafter, Whittier made his home in Amesbury and his important works were written there.

Whittier took a position in 1837, as a paid secretary for the American Anti-Slavery Society but quit this job on August 2, claiming there was too much work and it affected his heart trouble. The next month (September, 1837) he obtained a position as editor of the anti-slavery newspaper, the National Enquirer, published in Philadelphia, and after its name was changed to the Pennsylvania Freeman, he took full charge of it on March 15, 1838. On May 17, 1838, a pro-slavery mob burned the home of the Anti-Slavery Society, in Philadelphia, and also the offices of the Pennsylvania Freeman, which were in a part of that building. In 1841 the County paid the Society $33,000 as damages for the mob's work.

In October, 1838, an attack of nerves and heart trouble forced Whittier to return to his home in Amesbury, from whence he edited the Pennsylvania Freeman by mail until April, 1839; then he returned to Philadelphia and held his position until forced to resign, in 1840, as a result of a split over the policy of the Anti-Slavery Society. William Lloyd Garrison was the leader of a faction that wanted slavery abolished without further delay, even if it required the dissolution of the Union. Whittier was the leader of the faction that believed slavery would and could be abolished by political action under our Constitution and without the breaking-up of the Union. Garrison's faction controlled the Anti-Slavery Society and Whittier was forced to quit. He returned to his home in Amesbury a sick and disappointed man.

In the fall of 1840, Whittier was a candidate for Congress on the Liberal Party ticket but was defeated by Caleb Cushing seeking re-election as a Whig. In 1842, Whittier was again a candiate for Congress on the Liberal Party ticket and when the Whigs offered to support him, and his election appeared secure, Whittier withdrew from the contest, throwing his support to the Whig candidate so that he was elected.

From July 25, 1844, to March 13, 1845, Whittier was editor of the Middlesex Standard at Lowell, Mass. He lost this position when the newspaper was consolidated with a Worcester newspaper.

Whittier returned to Amesbury and "sold" the Amesbury Village Transcript the idea that it should be a county newspaper with Whittier as editor. The change was made, but the Essex Transcript was not a financial success and it soon returned to being the Village Transcript. It was during this year, 1846, that his aunt, Mercy Evans Hussey, died.

On January 1, 1847, Whittier became a corresponding editor for the National Era, a weekly published in Washington by the American and Foreign Anti-Slavery Society, which organization Whittier helped to form after his ouster from the American Anti-Slavery Society. He held this position until 1859.

During 1857, Whittier's mother died. From the first publishing of the Atlantic Monthly in 1857, he was a regular contributor to it. He was elected an overseer of Harvard University by the Massachusetts General Court in 1858 and, in 1860, Harvard gave him the honorary degree of master of arts. Whittier attended both the 1860 and 1864 conventions of the Republican party. During all of this period he was busy writing poetry and prose for the magazines and newspapers.

On September 3, 1864, his sister Elizabeth died. She had been an invalid for years and his constant companion and adviser. Whittier's niece, Elizabeth, the daughter of his brother Matthew Franklin Whittier, came to keep house for him. She remained with her uncle until 1876, when she married Samuel T. Pickard, who afterwards became Whittier's official biographer.

In 1869, Whittier was elected a trustee of Brown University, and in 1886 received the honorary degree of doctor of laws from Harvard. His health began to fail in 1888; in December, 1891, while visiting the Cartlands in Newburyport, he suffered an attack of the grippe; in June, 1892, he went to visit Miss Sarah Gove at her home, "Enfield," at Hampton Falls, N. H.; three months later, September 3, 1892, Whittier suffered a paralytic shock to his right side and died three days later, on September 6. His body is buried in the family lot in the Amesbury Cemetery on Route 110.

WHITTIER'S POETRY

John Greenleaf Whittier's poetry did more to create sentiment in favor of the abolition of slavery in our Country than the efforts of any other individual. He is rightfully called the "poet laureate of abolition." This volume contains a few of his many anti-slavery poems.

"The Farewell of a Virginia Slave Mother to Her Daughter Sold Into Southern Bondage" was published in 1838 and is claimed by many authorities to be the greatest of his anti-slavery poems—an inspired work.

"A Sabbath Scene" is one of Whittier's most melodramatic poems.

No other poet approached the heights that Whittier attained in his fight to rid our nation of slavery.

John Greenleaf Whittier's reputation as a poet is not based alone upon his anti-slavery poems, for his masterpiece is "Snow Bound," the greatest poem of its type written in the nineteenth century. "Barbara Frietchie" is a stirring and the best of modern ballads, his "At Last" is claimed by some authorities to be among the best devotional poems written outside the Book of Psalms.

"The Exile's Departure" was Whittier's first published poem; it appearing in William Lloyd Garrison's Newburyport Free Press on June 8, 1826, when Whittier was nineteen years of age.

"Snow Bound," his masterpiece, was written in 1865 when he was fifty-eight years of age.

The best known of his political poems is "Ichabod," written in 1850, in which he denounced Senator Daniel Webster for suggesting that the North concede on the slavery question to keep the South in the Union.

Among the Whittier narrative poems included in this selection are "Cassandra Southwick," "Women From Dover," "The Wreck at Rivermouth," "The Witch of Wenham," "Telling the Bees," "Kathleen," "Skipper Ireson's Ride," and "The Captain's Well."

THE EXILE'S DEPARTURE

This was the first of Whittier's poems to be published in a newspaper. It appeared on June 8, 1826, in William Lloyd Garrison's Newburyport Free Press.

Fond scenes, which delighted my youthful existence,
    With feelings of sorrow I bid ye adieu—
A lasting adieu! for now, dim in the distance,
    The shores of Hibernia recede from my view.
Farewell to the cliffs, tempest-beaten and gray,
    Which guard the lov'd shores of my own native land;
Farewell to the village and sail-shadow'd bay,
    The forest-crown'd hill and the water-wash'd strand.
I've fought for my country—I've brav'd all the dangers
    That throng round the path of the warrior in strife;
I now must depart to a nation of strangers,
    And pass in seclusion the remnant of life;
Far, far from the friends to my bosom most dear,
    With none to support me in peril and pain,
And none, but the stranger to drop the sad tear
    On the grave where the heart-broken Exile is lain.

Friends of my youth! I must leave you forever,
    And hasten to dwell in a region unknown:—
Yet time cannot change, nor the broad ocean sever,
    Hearts firmly united and tried as our own.
Ah, no! though I wander, all sad and forlorn,
    In a far distant land, yet shall memory trace,
When far o'er the ocean's white surges I'm borne,
    The scene of past pleasures,—my own native place.

Farewell, shores of Erin, green land of my fathers:—
    Once more, and forever, a mournful adieu!
For round thy dim headlands the ocean-mist gathers,
    And shrouds the fair isle I no longer can view.
I go—but wherever my footsteps I bend,
    For freedom and peace to my own native isle,
And contentment and joy to each warm-hearted friend
    Shall be the heart's prayer of the lonely Exile!

SNOW BOUND

The masterpiece. Published in 1865.

The sun that brief December day
Rose cheerless over hills of gray,
And, darkly circled, gave at noon
A sadder light than waning moon.
Slow tracing down the thickening sky
Its mute and ominous prophecy,
A portent seeming less than threat,
It sank from sight before it set.

A chill no coat, however stout,
Of homespun stuff could quite shut out,
A hard, dull bitterness of cold,
    That checked, mid-vein, the circling race
    Of life-blood in the sharpened face,
The coming of the snow-storm told.
The wind blew east; we heard the roar
Of Ocean on his wintry shore,
And felt the strong pulse throbbing there
Beat with low rhythm our inland air.

Meanwhile we did our nightly chores,—
Brought in the wood from out of doors,
Littered the stalls, and from the mows
Raked down the herd's grass for the cows:
Heard the horse whinnying for his corn;
And, sharply clashing horn on horn,
Impatient down the stanchion rows
The cattle shake their walnut bows;
While, peering from his early perch
Upon the scaffold's pole of birch,
The cock his crested helmet bent
And down his querulous challenge sent.
Unwarmed by any sunset light
The gray day darkened into night,
A night made hoary with the swarm,
And whirl-dance of the blinding storm,
As zigzag wavering to and fro
Crossed and recrossed the winged snow:
And ere the early bedtime came
The white drift piled the window-frame,
And through the glass the clothes-line posts
Looked in like tall and sheeted ghosts.

So all night long the storm roared on:
The morning broke without a sun;

In tiny spherule traced with lines
Of Nature's geometric signs,
In starry flake, and pellicle,
All day the hoary meteor fell;
And, when the second morning shone,
We looked upon a world unknown,
On nothing we could call our own.
Around the glistening wonder bent
The blue walls of the firmament,
No cloud above, no earth below,—
A universe of sky and snow!
The old familiar sights of ours
Took marvellous shapes, strange domes and towers
Rose up where sty or corn-crib stood,
Or garden-wall, or belt of wood;
A smooth white mound the brush-pile showed,
A fenceless drift what once was road;
The bridle-post an old man sat
With loose-flung coat and high cocked hat;
The well-curb had a Chinese roof;
And even the long sweep, high aloof,
In its slant splendor, seemed to tell
Of Pisa's leaning miracle.

A prompt, decisive man, no breath
Our father wasted: "Boys, a path!"
Well pleased, (for when did farmer boy
Count such a summons less than joy?)
Our buskins on our feet we drew;
   With mittened hands, and caps drawn low,
   To guard our necks and ears from snow,
We cut the solid whiteness through.
And, where the drift was deepest, made
A tunnel walled and overlaid
With dazzling crystal: we had read
Of rare Aladdin's wondrous cave,
And to our own his name we gave,
With many a wish the luck were ours
To test his lamp's supernal powers.
We reached the barn with merry din,
And roused the prisoned brutes within.
The old horse thrust his long head out,
And grave with wonder gazed about;
The cock his lusty greeting said,
And forth his speckled harem led;
The oxen lashed their tails, and hooked,
And mild reproach of hunger looked;
The horned patriarch of the sheep,

Like Egypt's Amun roused from sleep,
Shook his sage head with gesture mute,
And emphasized with stamp of foot.

All day the gusty north-wind bore
The loosening drift its breath before;
Low circling round its southern zone,
The sun through dazzling snow-mist shone.
No church-bell lent its Christian tone
To the savage air, no social smoke
Curled over woods of snow-hung oak.
A solitude made more intense
By dreary-voiced elements,
The shrieking of the mindless wind,
The moaning tree-boughs swaying blind,
And on the glass the unmeaning beat
Of ghostly finger-tips of sleet.
Beyond the circle of our hearth
No welcome sound of toil or mirth
Unbound the spell, and testified
Of human life and thought outside.
We minded that the sharpest ear
The buried brooklet could not hear,
The music of whose liquid lip
Had been to us companionship,
And, in our lonely life, had grown
To have an almost human tone.

As night drew on, and, from the crest
Of wooded knolls that ridged the west,
The sun, a snow-blown traveller, sank
From sight beneath the smothering bank,
We piled, with care, our nightly stack
Of wood against the chimney-back,—
The oaken log, green, huge, and thick,
And on its top the stout back-stick;
The knotty forestick laid apart,
And filled between with curious art
The ragged brush; then, hovering near,
We watched the first red blaze appear,
Heard the sharp crackle, caught the gleam
On whitewashed wall and sagging beam,
Until the old, rude-furnished room
Burst, flower-like, into rosy bloom;
While radiant with a mimic flame
Outside the sparkling drift became,
And through the bare-boughed lilac-tree
Our own warm hearth seemed blazing free.

SNOW BOUND

The crane and pendent trammels showed,
The Turks' heads on the andirons glowed;
While childish fancy, prompt to tell
The meaning of the miracle,
Whispered the old rhyme: "Under the tree,
When fire outdoors burns merrily,
There the witches are making tea."

The moon above the eastern wood
Shone at its full; the hill-range stood
Transfigured in the silver flood,
Its blown snows flashing cold and keen,
Dead white, save where some sharp ravine
Took shadow, or the sombre green
Of hemlocks turned to pitchy black
Against the whiteness at their back.
For such a world and such a night
Most fitting that unwarming light,
Which only seemed wher'er it fell
To make the coldness visible.
Shut in from all the world without,
We sat the clean-winged hearth about,
Content to let the north-wind roar
In baffled rage at pane and door,
While the red logs before us beat
The frost-line back with tropic heat;
And ever, when a louder blast
Shook beam and rafter as it passed,
The merrier up its roaring draught
The great throat of the chimney laughed,
The house-dog on his paws outspread
Laid to the fire his drowsy head,
The cat's dark silhouette on the wall
A couchant tiger's seemed to fall;
And, for the winter fireside meet,
Between the andirons' straddling feet,
The mug of cider simmered slow,
The apples sputtered in a row,
And, close at hand, the basket stood
With nuts from brown October's wood.

What matter how the night behaved?
What matter how the north-wind raved?
Blow high, blow low, not all its snow
Could quench our hearth-fire's ruddy glow.
O Time and Change!—with hair as gray
As was my sire's that winter day,
How strange it seems, with so much gone
Of life and love, to still live on!

Ah, brother! only I and thou
Are left of all that circle now,—
The dear home faces whereupon
That fitful firelight paled and shone.
Henceforward, listen as we will,
The voices of that hearth are still;
Look where we may, the wide earth o'er
Those lighted faces smile no more.
We tread the paths their feet have worn,
    We sit beneath their orchard trees,
    We hear, like them, the hum of bees
And rustle of the bladed corn;
We turn the pages that they read,
    Their written words we linger o'er,
But in the sun they cast no shade,
No voice is heard, no sign is made,
    No step is on the conscious floor!
Yet love will dream, and Faith will trust,
(Since He who knows our need is just,)
That somehow, somewhere, meet we must.
Alas for him who never sees
The stars shine through his cypress-trees!
Who, hopeless, lays his dead away,
Nor looks to see the breaking day
Across the mournful marbles play!
Who hath not learned, in hours of faith,
    The truth to flesh and sense unknown,
That Life is ever lord of Death,
    And Love can never lose its own!
We sped the time with stories old,
Wrought puzzles out, and riddles told,
Or stammered from our school-book lore
"The Chief of Gambia's golden shore."
How often since, when all the land
Was clay in Slavery's shaping hand,
As if a trumpet called, I've heard
Dame Mercy Warren's rousing word:
"Does not the voice of reason cry,
    Claim the first right which Nature gave,
From the red scourge of bondage fly,
    Nor deign to live a burdened slave."
Our father rode again his ride
On Memphremagog's wooded side;
Sat down again to moose and samp
In trapper's hut and Indian camp;
Lived o'er the old idyllic ease
Beneath St. Francois' hemlock-trees;
Again for him the moonlight shone

SNOW BOUND

On Norman cap and bodiced zone;
Again we heard the violin play
Which led the village dance away,
And mingled in its merry whirl
The grandam and the laughing girl.
Or, nearer home, our steps he led
Where Salisbury's level marshes spread
    Mile-wide as flies the laden bee;
Where merry mowers, hale and strong,
Swept, scythe on scythe, their swaths along
    The low green prairies of the sea.
We shared the fishing off Boar's Head,
    And round the rocky Isles of Shoals
    The hake-broil on the drift-wood coals;
The chowder on the sand-beach made,
Dipped by the hungry, steaming hot,
With spoons of clam-shell from the pot.
We heard the tales of witchcraft old,
And dream and sign and marvel told
To sleepy listeners as they lay
Stretched idly on the salted hay,
Adrift along the winding shores,
When favoring breezes deigned to blow
The square sail of the gundelow
And idle lay the useless oars.

Our mother, while she turned her wheel
Or run the new-knit stocking-heel,
Told how the Indian hordes came down
At midnight on Cocheco town,
And how her own great-uncle bore
His cruel scalp-mark to fourscore.
Recalling, in her fitting phrase,
    So rich and picturesque and free,
    (The common unrhymed poetry
Of simple life and country ways,)
The story of her early days,—
She made us welcome to her home;
Old hearths grew wide to give us room;
We stole with her a frightened look
At the gray wizard's conjuring-book,
The fame whereof went far and wide
Through all the simple country side;
We heard the hawks at twilight play,
The boat-horn on Piscataqua,
The loon's weird laughter far away;
We fished her little trout-brook, knew
What flowers in wood and meadow grew,

What sunny hillsides autumn-brown
She climbed to shake the ripe nuts down,
Saw where in sheltered cove and bay
The ducks' black squadron anchored lay,
And heard the wild geese calling loud
Beneath the gray November cloud.

Then, haply, with a look more grave,
And soberer tone, some tale she gave
From painful Sewel's ancient tome,
Beloved in every Quaker home,
Of faith fire-winged by martyrdom,
Or Chalkley's Journal, old and quaint,—
Gentlest of skippers, rare sea-saint!—
Who, when the dreary calms prevailed,
And water-butt and bread-cask failed,
And cruel, hungry eyes pursued
His portly presence mad for food,
With dark hints muttered under breath
Of casting lots for life or death,
Offered, if Heaven withheld supplies,
To be himself the sacrifice.
Then, suddenly, as if to save
The good man from his living grave,
A ripple on the water grew,
A school of porpoise flashed in view.
"Take, eat," he said, "and be content;
These fishes in my stead are sent
By Him who gave the tangled ram
To spare the child of Abraham."

Our uncle, innocent of books,
Was rich in lore of fields and brooks,
The ancient teachers never dumb
Of Nature's unhoused lyceum.
In moons and tides and weather wise,
He read the clouds as prophecies,
And foul or fair could well divine,
By many an occult hint and sign,
Holding the cunning-warded keys
To call the woodcraft mysteries;
Himself to Nature's heart so near
That all her voices in his ear
Of beast or bird had meanings clear,
Like Apollonius of old,
Who knew the tales the sparrows told,
Or Hermes who interpreted
What the sage cranes of Nilus said;

SNOW BOUND

A simple, guileless, childlike man,
Content to live where life began;
Strong only on his native grounds,
The little world of sights and sounds
Whose girdle was the parish bounds,
Whereof his fondly partial pride
The common features magnified,
As Surrey hills to mountains grew
In White of Selborne's loving view,—
He told how teal and loon he shot,
And how the eagle's eggs he got,
The feats on pond and river done,
The prodigies of rod and gun;
Till, warming with the tales he told,
Forgotten was the outside cold,
The bitter wind unheeded blew,
From ripening corn the pigeons flew,
The partridge drummed i' the wood, the mink
Went fishing down the river-brink.
In fields with bean or clover gay,
The woodchuck, like a hermit gray,
    Peered from the doorway of his cell;
The muskrat plied the mason's trade,
And tier by tier his mud-walls laid;
And from the shagbark overhead
    The grizzled squirrel dropped his shell.

    Next, the dear aunt, whose smile of cheer
And voice in dreams I see and hear,—
The sweetest women ever Fate
Perverse denied a household mate,
Who, lonely, homeless, not the less
Found peace in love's unselfishness,
And welcome wheresoe'er she went,
A calm and gracious element,
Whose presence seemed the sweet income
And womanly atmosphere of home,—
Called up her girlhood memories,
The huskings and the apple-bees,
The sleigh-rides and the summer sails,
Weaving through all the poor details
And homespun warp of circumstance
A golden woof-thread of romance.
For well she kept her genial mood
And simple faith of maidenhood;
Before her still a cloud-land lay,
The mirage loomed across her way;
The morning dew, that dries so soon
With others, glistened at her noon;

Through years of toil and soil and care,
From glossy tress to thin gray hair,
All unprofaned she held apart
The virgin fancies of the heart.
Be shame to him of woman born
Who hath for such but thought of scorn.

There, too, our elder sister plied
Her evening task the stand beside;
A full, rich nature, free to trust,
Truthful and almost sternly just,
Impulsive, earnest, prompt to act,
And make her generous thought a fact,
Keeping with many a light disguise
The secret of self-sacrifice.
O heart sore-tried! thou hast the best
That Heaven itself could give thee—rest,
Rest from all bitter thoughts and things!
    How many a poor one's blessing went
    With thee beneath the low green tent
Whose curtain never outward swings!

As one who held herself a part
Of all she saw, and let her heart
    Against the household bosom lean,
Upon the motley-braided mat
Our youngest and our dearest sat,
Lifting her large, sweet, asking eyes,
    Now bathed within the fadeless green
And holy peace of Paradise.
O, looking from some heavenly hill,
    Or from the shade of saintly palms,
    Or silver reach of river calms,
Do those large eyes behold me still?
With me one little year ago:—
The chill weight of the winter snow
    For months upon her grave has lain;
And now, when summer south-winds blow
    And brier and harebell bloom again,
I tread the pleasant paths we trod,
I see the violet-sprinkled sod
Whereon she leaned, too frail and weak
The hillside flowers she loved to seek,
Yet following me where'er I went
With dark eyes full of love's content.
The birds are glad; the brier-rose fills
The air with sweetness; all the hills
Stretch green to June's unclouded sky;

But still I wait with ear and eye
For something gone which should be nigh,
A loss in all familiar things,
In flower that blooms, and bird that sings.
And yet, dear heart! remembering thee,
    Am I not richer than of old?
Safe in thy immortality,
    What change can reach the wealth I hold?
    What chance can mar the pearl and gold
Thy love hath left in trust with me?
And while in life's late afternoon,
    Where cool and long the shadows grow,
I walk to meet the night that soon
    Shall shape and shadow overflow,
I cannot feel that thou art far,
Since near at need the angels are;
And when the sunset gates unbar,
    Shall I not see thee waiting stand,
And, white against the evening star,
    The welcome of thy beckoning hand?

Brisk wielder of the birch and rule,
The master of the district school
Held at the fire his favored place,
Its warm glow lit a laughing face
Fresh-hued and fair, where scarce appeared
The uncertain prophecy of beard.
He teased the mitten-blinded cat,
Played cross-pins on my uncle's hat,
Sang songs, and told us what befalls
In classic Dartmouth's college halls.
Born the wild Northern hills among,
From whence his yeoman father wrung
By patient toil subsistence scant,
Not competence and yet not want,
He early gained the power to pay
His cheerful, self-reliant way;
Could doff at ease his scholar's gown
To peddle wares from town to town;
Or through the long vacation's reach
In lonely lowland districts teach,
Where all the droll experience found
At stranger hearths in boarding round,
The moonlit skater's keen delight,
The sleigh-drive through the frosty night,
The rustic party, with its rough
Accompaniment of blind-man's-buff,
And whirling plate, and forfeits paid,

His winter task a pastime made.
Happy the snow-locked homes wherein
He tuned his merry violin,
Or played the athlete in the barn,
Or held the good dame's winding-yarn,
Or mirth-provoking versions told
Of classic legends rare and old,
Wherein the scenes of Greece and Rome
Had all the commonplace of home,
And little seemed at best the odds
'Twixt Yankee pedlers and old gods;
Where Pindus-born Araxes took
The guise of any grist-mill brook;
And dread Olympus at his will
Became a huckleberry hill.

A careless boy that night he seemed;
    But at his desk he had the look
And air of one who wisely schemed,
    And hostage from the future took
      In trained thought and lore of book.
Large-brained, clear-eyed,—of such as he
Shall Freedom's young apostles be,
Who, following in War's bloody trail,
Shall every lingering wrong assail;
All chains from limb and spirit strike,
Uplift the black and white alike;
Scatter before their swift advance
The darkness and the ignorance,
The pride, the lust, the squalid sloth,
Which nurtured Treason's monstrous growth,
Made murder pastime, and the hell
Of prison-torture possible;
The cruel lie of caste refute,
Old forms remould, and substitute
For Slavery's lash the freeman's will,
For blind routine, wise-handed skill;
A school-house plant on every hill,
Stretching in radiate nerve-lines thence
The quick wires of intelligence;
Till North and South together brought
Shall own the same electric thought,
In peace a common flag salute,
And, side by side in labor's free
And unresentful rivalry,
Harvest the fields wherein they fought.

SNOW BOUND

Another guest that winter night
Flashed back from lustrous eyes the light.
Unmarked by time, and yet not young,
The honeyed music of her tongue
And words of meekness scarcely told
A nature passionate and bold,
Strong, self-concentrated, spurning guide,
Its milder features dwarfed beside
Her unbent will's majestic pride.
She sat among us, at the best,
A not unfeared, half-welcome guest,
Rebuking with her cultured phrase
Our homeliness of words and ways.
A certain pard-like, treacherous grace
    Swayed the lithe limbs and dropped the lash,
    Lent the white teeth their dazzling flash;
    And under low brows, black with night,
    Rayed out at times a dangerous light;
The sharp heat-lightnings of her face
Presaging ill to him whom Fate
Condemned to share her love or hate.
A woman tropical, intense
In thought and act, in soul and sense,
She blended in a like degree
The vixen and the devotee,
Revealing with each freak or feint
    The temper of Petruchio's Kate,
The raptures of Siena's saint.
Her tapering hand and rounded wrist
Had facile power to form a fist;
The warm, dark languish of her eyes
Was never safe from wrath's surprise.
Brows saintly calm and lips devout
Knew every change of scowl and pout;
And the sweet voice had notes more high
And shrill for social battle-cry.

Since then what old cathedral town
Has missed her pilgrim staff and gown,
What convent-gate has held its lock
Against the challenge of her knock!
Through Smyrna's plague-hushed thoroughfares,
Up sea-set Malta's rocky stairs,
Gray olive slopes of hills that hem
Thy tombs and shrines, Jerusalem,
Or startling on her desert throne
The crazy Queen of Lebanon
With claims fantastic as her own,

Her tireless feet have held their way;
And still, unrestful, bowed, and gray,
She watches under Eastern skies,
    With hope each day renewed and fresh,
    The Lord's quick coming in the flesh,
Whereof she dreams and prophesies!

Where'er her troubled path may be,
    The Lord's sweet pity with her go!
The outward wayward life we see,
    The hidden springs we may not know.
Nor is it given us to discern
    What threads the fatal sisters spun,
    Through what ancestral years has run
The sorrow with the woman born,
What forged her cruel chain of moods,
What set her feet in solitudes,
    And held the love within her mute,
What mingled madness in the blood,
    A life-long discord and annoy,
    Water of tears with oil of joy,
And hid within the folded bud
    Perversities of flower and fruit.
It is not ours to separate
The tangled skein of will and fate,
To show what metes and bounds should stand
Upon the soul's debatable land,
And between choice and Providence
Divide the circle of events;
    But He who knows our frame is just,
Merciful and compassionate,
And full of sweet assurances
And hope for all the language is,
    That He remembereth we are dust!

At last the great logs, crumbling low,
Sent out a dull and duller glow,
The bull's-eye watch that hung in view,
Ticking its weary circuit through,
Pointed with mutely warning sign
Its black hand to the hour of nine.
That sign the pleasant circle broke:
My uncle ceased his pipe to smoke,
Knocked from its bowl the refuse gray,
And laid it tenderly away,
Then roused himself to safely cover
The dull red brands with ashes over.
And while, with care, our mother laid

SNOW BOUND

The work aside, her steps she stayed
One moment, seeking to express
Her grateful sense of happiness
For food and shelter, warmth and health,
And love's contentment more than wealth,
With simple wishes (not the weak,
Vain prayers which no fulfillment seek,
But such as warm the generous heart,
O'er-prompt to do with Heaven its part)
That none might lack, that bitter night,
For bread and clothing, warmth and light.

Within our beds awhile we heard
The wind that round the gables roared,
With now and then a ruder shock,
Which made our very bedsteads rock.
We heard the loosened clapboards tost,
The board-nails snapping in the frost;
And on us, through the unplastered wall,
Felt the light sifted snow-flakes fall.
But sleep stole on, as sleep will do
When hearts are light and life is new;
Faint and more faint the murmurs grew,
Till in the summer-land of dreams
They softened to the sound of streams,
Low stir of leaves, and dip of oars,
And lapsing waves on quiet shores.

Next morn we wakened with the shout
Of merry voices high and clear;
And saw the teamsters drawing near
To break the drifted highways out.
Down the long hillside treading slow
We saw the half-buried oxen go,
Shaking the snow from heads uptost,
Their straining nostrils white with frost.
Before our door the straggling train
Drew up, an added team to gain.
The elders threshed their hands a-cold,
    Passed, with the cider-mug, their jokes
From lip to lip; the younger folks
Down the loose snow-banks, wrestling, rolled,
Then toiled again the cavalcade
    O'er windy hill, through clogged ravine,
    And woodland paths that wound between
Low drooping pine-boughs winter-weighed.
From every barn a team afoot,
At every house a new recruit,

Where, drawn by Nature's subtlest law
Haply the watchful young men saw
Sweet doorway pictures of the curls
And curious eyes of merry girls,
Lifting their hands in mock defence
Against the snow-ball's compliments,
And reading in each missive tost
The charm with Eden never lost.

We heard once more the sleigh-bells' sound;
    And, following where the teamsters led,
The wise old Doctor went his round,
Just pausing at our door to say,
In the brief autocratic way
Of one who, prompt at Duty's call,
Was free to urge her claim on all,
    That some poor neighbor sick abed
At night our mother's aid would need.
For, one in generous thought and deed,
    What mattered in the sufferer's sight
    The Quaker matron's inward light,
The Doctor's mail of Calvin's creed?
All hearts confess the saints elect
    Who, twain in faith, in love agree,
And melt not in an acid sect
    The Christian pearl of charity!

So days went on: a week had passed
Since the great world was heard from last.
The Almanac we studied o'er,
Read and reread our little store,
Of books and pamphlets, scarce a score;
One harmless novel, mostly hid
From younger eyes, a book forbid,
And poetry, (or good or bad,
A single book was all we had,)
Where Ellwood's meek, drab-skirted Muse,
    A stranger to the heathen Nine,
    Sang, with a somewhat nasal whine,
The wars of David and the Jews.
At last the floundering carrier bore
The village paper to our door.
Lo! broadening outward as we read,
To warmer zones the horizon spread;
In panoramic length unrolled
We saw the marvels that it told.
Before us passed the painted Creeks,

SNOW BOUND

And daft McGregor on his raids
In Costa Rica's everglades.
And up Taygetos winding slow
Rode Ypsilanti's Mainote Greeks,
A Turk's head at each saddle-bow!
Welcome to us its week-old news,
Its corner for the rustic Muse,
Its monthly gauge of snow and rain,
Its record, mingling in a breath
The wedding bell and dirge of death;
Jest, anecdote, and love-lorn tale,
The latest culprit sent to jail;
Its hue and cry of stolen and lost,
Its vendue sales and goods at cost,
And traffic calling loud for gain.
We felt the stir of hall and street,
The pulse of life that round us beat;
The chill embargo of the snow
Was melted in the genial glow;
Wide swung again our ice-locked door,
And all the world was ours once more;

Clasp, Angel of the backward look
And folded wings of ashen gray
And voice of echoes far away,
The brazen covers of thy book;
The weird palimpset old and vast,
Wherein thou hid'st the spectral past;
Where, closely mingling, pale and glow
The characters of joy and woe;
The monographs of outlived years,
Or smile-illumed or dim with tears,
Green hills of life that slope to death,
And haunts of home, whose vistaed trees
Shade off to mournful cypresses
With the white amaranths underneath.
Even while I look, I can but heed
The restless sands' incessant fall,
Importunate hours that hours succeed,
Each clamorous with its own sharp need,
And duty keeping pace with all.
Shut down and clasp the heavy lids;
I hear again the voice that bids
The dreamer leave his dream midway
For larger hopes and graver fears:
Life greatens in these later years,
The century's aloe flowers to-day!

Yet, haply, in some lull of life,
Some Truce of God which breaks its strife,
The worldling's eyes shall gather dew,
    Dreaming in throngful city ways
Of winter joys his boyhood knew;
And dear and early friends—the few
Who yet remain—shall pause to view
    These Flemish pictures of old days;
Sit with me by the homestead hearth,
And stretch the hands of memory forth
    To warm them at the wood-fire's blaze!
And thanks untraced to lips unknown
Shall greet me like the odors blown
From unseen meadows newly mown,
Or lilies floating in some pond,
Wood-fringed, the wayside gaze beyond;
The traveller owns the grateful sense
Of sweetness near, he knows not whence,
And, pausing, takes with forehead bare
The benediction of the air.

BARBARA FRIETCHIE

Mrs. E. D. E. A. Southworth, then America's leading novelist, supplied Whittier with the facts upon which this poem is based. It is now claimed by some that the flag was displayed before the Confederate soldiers by a Mrs. Quantrell and that Barbara Frietchie was only an onlooker; others contend that it was Barbara Frietchie that waved the flag and dared Stonewall Jackson to shoot her; as the poem was written in 1863 and, as it is the tendency of some always to claim the credit due others, the probabilities are that Whittier knew the facts when he wrote the poem.

Up from the meadows rich with corn,
Clear in the cool September morn,

The clustered spires of Frederick stand
Green-walled by the hills of Maryland.

Round about them orchards sweep,
Apple and peach tree fruited deep,

Fair as the garden of the Lord
To the eyes of the famished rebel horde,

On that pleasant morn of the early fall
When Lee marched over the mountain-wall,—

BARBARA FRIETCHIE

Over the mountains winding down,
Horse and foot, into Frederick town.

Forty flags with their silver stars,
Forty flags with their crimson bars,

Flapped in the morning wind: the sun
Of noon looked down, and saw not one.

Up rose old Barbara Frietchie then,
Bowed with her fourscore years and ten;

Bravest of all in Frederick town,
She took up the flag the men hauled down;

In her attic window the staff she set,
To show that one heart was loyal yet.

Up the street came the rebel tread,
Stonewall Jackson riding ahead.

Under his slouched hat left and right
He glanced: the old flag met his sight.

"Halt!"—the dust-brown ranks stood fast.
"Fire!"—out blazed the rifle-blast.

It shivered the window, pane and sash;
It rent the banner with seam and gash.

Quick, as it fell, from the broken staff
Dame Barbara snatched the silken scarf.

She leaned far out on the window-sill,
And shook it forth with a royal will.

"Shoot, if you must, this old gray head,
But spare your country's flag," she said.

A shade of sadness, a blush of shame,
Over the face of the leader came;

The nobler nature within him stirred
To life at that woman's deed and word:

"Who touches a hair of yon gray head
Dies like a dog! March on!" he said.

All day long through Frederick Street
Sounded the tread of marching feet:

All day long that free flag tost
Over the heads of the rebel host.

Ever its torn folds rose and fell
On the loyal winds that loved it well;

And through the hill-gaps sunset light
Shone over it with a warm good-night.

Barbara Frietchie's work is o'er,
And the Rebel rides on his raids no more.

Honor to her! and let a tear
Fall, for her sake, on Stonewall's bier.

Over Barbara Frietchie's grave,
Flag of Freedom and Union, wave!

Peace and order and beauty draw
Round thy symbol of light and law;

And ever the stars above look down
On thy stars below in Frederick town!

THE BAREFOOT BOY
1855

Blessings on thee, little man,
Barefoot boy, with cheek of tan!
With thy turned-up pantaloons,
And thy merry whistled tunes;
With thy red lip, redder still
Kissed by strawberries on the hill;
With the sunshine on thy face,
Through thy torn brim's jaunty grace;
From my heart I give thee joy,—
I was once a barefoot boy!
Prince thou art,—the grown-up man
Only is republican.
Let the million-dollared ride!
Barefoot, trudging at his side,
Thou hast more than he can buy
In the reach of ear and eye,—
Outward sunshine, inward joy:
Blessings on thee, barefoot boy!

O for boyhood's painless play,
Sleep that wakes in laughing day,
Health that mocks the doctor's rules,
Knowledge never learned of schools,
Of the wild bee's morning chase,
Of the wild-flower's time and place,
Flight of fowl and habitude
Of the tenants of the wood;
How the tortoise bears his shell,
How the woodchuck digs his cell,

THE BAREFOOT BOY

And the ground-mole sinks his well;
How the robin feeds her young,
How the oriole's nest is hung;
Where the whitest lilies blow,
Where the freshest berries grow,
Where the groundnut trails its vine,
Where the wood-grape's clusters shine;
Of the black wasp's cunning way,
Mason of his walls of clay,
And the architectural plans
Of gray hornet artisans!—
For, eschewing books and tasks,
Nature answers all he asks;
Hand in hand with her he walks,
Face to face with her he talks,
Part and parcel of her joy,—
Blessings on the barefoot boy!

O for boyhood's time of June,
Crowding years in one brief moon,
When all things I heard or saw,
Me, their master, waited for.
I was rich in flowers and trees,
Humming-birds and honey-bees;
For my sport the squirrel played,
Plied the snouted mole his spade;
For my taste the blackberry cone
Purpled over hedge and stone;
Laughed the brook for my delight
Through the day and through the night,
Whispering at the garden wall,
Talked with me from fall to fall;
Mine the sand-rimmed pickerel pond,
Mine the walnut slopes beyond,
Mine, on bending orchard trees,
Apples of Hesperides!
Still as my horizon grew,
Larger grew my riches too,
All the world I saw or knew
Seemed a complex Chinese toy,
Fashioned for a barefoot boy!

O for festal dainties spread,
Like my bowl of milk and bread,—
Pewter spoon and bowl of wood,
On the door-stone, gray and rude!
O'er me, like a regal tent,
Cloudy-ribbed, the sunset bent,

Purple-curtained, fringed with gold,
Looped in many a wind-swung fold;
While for music came the play
Of the pied frogs' orchestra;
And, to light the noisy choir,
Lit the fly his lamp of fire.
I was monarch: pomp and joy
Waited on the barefoot boy!

Cherrily, then, my little man,
Live and laugh, as boyhood can!
Though the flinty slopes be hard,
Stubble-speared the new-mown sward,
Every morn shall lead thee through
Fresh baptisms of the dew;
Every evening from thy feet
Shall the cool wind kiss the heat:
All too soon these feet must hide
In the prison cells of pride,
Lose the freedom of the sod,
Like a colt's for work be shod,
Made to tread the mills of toil,
Up and down in ceaseless moil:
Happy if their track be found
Never on forbidden ground;
Happy if they sink not in
Quick and treacherous sands of sin.
Ah! that thou couldst know thy joy,
Ere it passes, barefoot boy!

MAUD MULLER
1855

MAUD MULLER, on a summer's day,
Raked the meadow sweet with hay.

Beneath her torn hat glowed the wealth
Of simple beauty and rustic health.

Singing, she wrought, and her merry glee
The mock-bird echoed from his tree.

But when she glanced to the far-off town,
White from its hill-slope looking down,

The sweet song died, and a vague unrest
And a nameless longing filled her breast,—

A wish, that she hardly dared to own,
For something better than she had known.

The Judge rode slowly down the lane,
Smoothing his horse's chestnut mane.

He drew his bridle in the shade
Of the apple-trees, to greet the maid,

And asked a draught from the spring that flowed
Through the meadow across the road.

She stooped where the cool spring bubbled up,
And filled for him her small tin cup,

And blushed as she gave it, looking down
On her feet so bare, and her tattered gown.

"Thanks!" said the Judge; "a sweeter draught
From a fairer hand was never quaffed."

He spoke of the grass and flowers and trees,
Of the singing birds and the humming bees;

Then talked of the haying, and wondered whether
The cloud in the west would bring foul weather.

And Maud forgot her brier-torn gown,
And her graceful ankles bare and brown;

And listened, while a pleased surprise
Looked from her long-lashed hazel eyes.

At last, like one who for delay
Seeks a vain excuse, he rode away.

Maud Muller looked and sighed: "Ah me!
That I the Judge's bride might be!

"He would dress me up in silks so fine,
And praise and toast me at his wine.

"My father should wear a broadcloth coat;
My brother should sail a painted boat.

"I'd dress my mother so grand and gay,
And the baby should have a new toy each day.

"And I'd feed the hungry and clothe the poor,
And all should bless me who left our door."

The Judge looked back as he climbed the hill,
And saw Maud Muller standing still.

"A form more fair, a face more sweet,
Ne'er hath it been my lot to meet.

"And her modest answer and graceful air
Show her wise and good as she is fair.

"Would she were mine, and I today,
Like her, a harvester of hay:

"No doubtful balance of rights and wrongs,
Nor weary lawyers with endless tongues,

"But low of cattle and song of birds,
And health and quiet and loving words."

But he thought of his sisters, proud and cold,
And his mother, vain of her rank and gold.

So, closing his heart, the Judge rode on,
And Maud was left in the field alone.

But the lawyer smiled that afternoon,
When he hummed in court an old love-tune;

And the young girl mused beside the well
Till the rain on the unraked clover fell.

He wedded a wife of richest dower,
Who lived for fashion, as he for power.

Yet oft, in his marble hearth's bright glow,
He watched a picture come and go;

And sweet Maud Muller's hazel eyes
Looked out in their innocent surprise.

Oft, when the wine in his glass was red,
He longed for the wayside well instead;

And closed his eyes on his garnished rooms
To dream of meadows and clover-blooms.

And the proud man sighed, with a secret pain,
"Ah, that I were free again!

"Free as when I rode that day,
Where the barefoot maiden raked her hay."

She wedded a man unlearned and poor,
And many children played round her door.

But care and sorrow, and childbirth pain,
Left their traces on heart and brain,

And oft, when the summer sun shone hot
On the new-mown hay in the meadow lot,

And she heard the little spring brook fall
Over the roadside, through the wall,

In the shade of the apple-tree again
She saw a rider draw his rein.

And, gazing down with timid grace,
She felt his pleased eyes read her face.

Sometimes her narrow kitchen walls
Stretched away into stately halls;

The weary wheel to a spinnet turned,
The tallow candle an astral burned,

And for him who sat by the chimney lug,
Dozing and grumbling o'er pipe and mug,

A manly form at her side she saw,
And joy was duty and love was law.

Then she took up her burden of life again,
Saying only, "It might have been."

Alas for maiden, alas for Judge,
For rich repiner and household drudge!

God pity them both! and pity us all,
Who vainly the dreams of youth recall.

For of all sad words of tongue or pen,
The saddest are these: "It might have been!"

Ah, well! for us all some sweet hope lies
Deeply buried from human eyes;

And, in the hereafter, angels may
Roll the stone from its grave away!

MEMORIES

A beautiful and happy girl,
    With step as light as summer air,
Eyes glad with smiles, and brow of pearl,
Shadowed by many a careless curl
    Of unconfined and flowing hair;
A seeming child in everything,
    Save thoughtful brow and ripening charms,
As Nature wears the smile of Spring
    When sinking into Summer's arms.

A mind rejoicing in the light
    Which melted through its graceful bower,
Leaf after leaf, dew-moist and bright,
And stainless in its holy white,
    Unfolding like a morning flower:
A heart, which, like a fine-toned lute,
    With every breath of feeling woke,
And, even when the tongue was mute,
    From eye and lip in music spoke.

How thrills once more the lengthening chain
    Of memory, at the thought of thee!
Old hopes which long in dust have lain
Old dreams, come thronging back again,
    And boyhood lives again in me;
I feel its glow upon my cheek,
    Its fulness of the heart is mine,
As when I learned to hear thee speak,
    Or raised my doubtful eye to thine.

I hear again thy low replies,
    I feel thy arm within my own,
And timidly again uprise
The fringed lids of hazel eyes,
    With soft brown tresses overblown.
Ah! memories of sweet summer eves,
    Of moonlit wave and willowy way,
Of stars and flowers, and dewy leaves,
    And smiles and tones more dear than they!

Ere this, thy quiet eye hath smiled
    My picture of thy youth to see,
When, half a woman, half a child,
Thy very artlessness beguiled,
    And folly's self seemed wise in thee;
I too can smile, when o'er that hour
    The lights of memory backward stream,
Yet feel the while that manhood's power
    Is vainer than my boyhood's dream.

Years have passed on, and left their trace,
    Of graver care and deeper thought;
And unto me the calm, cold face
Of manhood, and to thee the grace
    Of woman's pensive beauty brought.
More wide, perchance, for blame than praise,
    The school-boy's humble name has flown;
Thine, in the green and quiet ways
    Of unobtrusive goodness known.

And wider yet in thought and deed
    Diverge our pathways, one in youth;
Thine the Genevan's sternest creed,
While answers to my spirit's need
    The Derby dalesman's simple truth.
For thee, the priestly rite and prayer,
    And holy day, and solemn psalm;
For me, the silent reverence where
    My brethren gather, slow and calm.

IN SCHOOL DAYS

Yet hath thy spirit left on me
 An impress Time has worn not out,
And something of myself in thee,
 A shadow from the past, I see,
  Lingering, even yet, thy way about;
Not wholly can the heart unlearn
 That lesson of its better hours,
Not yet has Time's dull footstep worn
 To common dust that path of flowers.

Thus, while at times before our eyes
 The shadows melt, and fall apart,
And, smiling through them, round us lies
The warm light of our morning skies,—
 The Indian Summer of the heart!—
In secret sympathies of mind,
 In founts of feeling which retain
Their pure, fresh flow, we yet may find
 Our early dreams not wholly vain!

IN SCHOOL DAYS

Written in memory of Lydia Ayer, Whittier's boyhood sweetheart. Lydia, the daughter of a neighbor, Captain William Ayer, died when she was only fourteen and is buried in the Walnut Cemetery, Kenoza Street, in the East Parish of Haverhill (off Route 110). Of this poem, Oliver Wendell Holmes wrote to Whittier, "You have written the finest schoolboy poem in the English language."

Still sits the school-house by the road,
 A ragged beggar sunning;
Around it still the sumachs grow,
 And blackberry-vines are running.

Within, the master's desk is seen,
 Deep scarred by raps official;
The warping floor, the battered seats,
 The jack-knife's carved initial;

The charcoal frescos on its wall;
 Its door's worn sill, betraying
The feet that, creeping slow to school,
 Went storming out to playing!

Long years ago a winter sun
 Shone over it at setting;
Lit up its western window-panes,
 And low eaves' icy fretting.

It touched the tangled golden curls,
    And brown eyes full of grieving,
Of one who still her steps delayed
    When all the school were leaving.

For near her stood the little boy
    Her childish favor singled:
His cap pulled low upon a face
    Where pride and shame were mingled.

Pushing with restless feet the snow
    To right and left, he lingered;—
As restlessly her tiny hands
    The blue-checked apron fingered.

He saw her lift her eyes; he felt
    The soft hand's light caressing,
And heard the tremble of her voice,
    As if a fault confessing.

"I'm sorry that I spelt the word:
    I hate to go above you,
Because, "—the brown eyes lower fell,—
    "Because, you see, I love you!"

Still memory to a gray-haired man
    That sweet child-face is showing.
Dear girl! the grasses on her grave
    Have forty years been growing!

He lives to learn, in life's hard school,
    How few who pass above him
Lament their triumph and his loss,
    Like her,—because they love him.

THE COUNTESS

Written in memory of Mary Ingalls, the wife of Count Francis Vipart of Guadaloupe, the first American girl to marry a title. She died January 5th, 1807, and is buried in the Greenwood Cemetery on East Broadway, in Haverhill (off Route 110).

I know not, Time and Space so intervene,
Whether, still waiting with a trust serene,
Thou bearest up thy fourscore years and ten,
Or, called at last, art now Heaven's citizen;
But, here or there, a pleasant thought of thee,
Like an old friend, all day has been with me.

THE COUNTESS

The shy, still boy, for whom thy kindly hand
Smoothed his hard pathway to the wonder-land
Of thought and fancy, in gray manhood yet
Keeps green the memory of his early debt.
To-day, when truth and falsehood speak their words
Through hot-lipped cannon and the teeth of swords,
Listening with quickened heart and ear intent
To each sharp clause of that stern argument,
I still can hear at times a softer note
Of the old pastoral music round me float,
While through the hot gleam of our civil strife
Looms the green mirage of a simpler life.
As, at his alien post, the sentinel
Drops the old bucket in the homestead well,
And hears old voices in the winds that toss
Above his head the live-oak's beard of moss,
So, in our trial-time, and under skies
Shadowed by swords like Islam's paradise,
I wait and watch, and let my fancy stray
To milder scenes and youth's Arcadian day;
And howsoe'er the pencil dipped in dreams
Shades the brown woods or tints the sunset streams,
The country doctor in the foreground seems,
Whose ancient sulky down the village lanes
Dragged, like a war-car, captive ills and pains.
I could not paint the scenery of my song,
Mindless of one who looked thereon so long;
Who, night and day, on duty's lonely round,
Made friends o' the woods and rocks, and knew the sound
Of each small brook, and what the hill-side trees
Said to the winds that touched their leafy keys;
Who saw so keenly and so well could paint
The village-folk, with all their humors quaint,—
The parson ambling on his wall-eyed roan,
Grave and erect, with white hair backward blown;
The tough old boatman, half amphibious grown;
The muttering witch-wife of the gossip's tale,
And the loud straggler levying his black-mail,—
Old customs, habits, superstitions, fears,
All that lies buried under fifty years.
To thee, as is most fit, I bring my lay,
And, grateful, own the debt I cannot pay.

    Over the wooded northern ridge,
        Between its houses brown,
   To the dark tunnel of the bridge
        The street comes straggling down.

You catch a glimpse, through birch and pine,
    Of gable, roof, and porch,
The tavern with its swinging sign,
    The sharp horn of the church.

The river's steel-blue crescent curves
    To meet, in ebb and flow,
The single broken wharf that serves
    For sloop and gundelow.

With salt sea-scents along its shores
    The heavy hay-boats crawl,
The long antennae of their oars
    In lazy rise and fall.

Along the gray abutment's wall
    The idle shad-net dries;
The toll-man in his cobbler's stall
    Sits smoking with closed eyes.

You hear the pier's low undertone
    Of waves that chafe and gnaw;
You start,—a skipper's horn is blown
    To raise the creaking draw.

At times a blacksmith's anvil sounds
    With slow and sluggard beat,
Or stage-coach on its dusty rounds
    Wakes up the staring street.

A place for idle eyes and ears,
    A cobwebbed nook of dreams;
Left by the stream whose waves are years
    The stranded village seems.

And there, like other moss and rust,
    The native dweller clings,
And keeps, in uninquiring trust,
    The old, dull round of things.

The fisher drops his patient lines,
    The farmer sows his grain,
Content to hear the murmuring pines
    Instead of railroad-train.

Go where, along the tangled steep
    That slopes against the west,
The hamlet's buried idlers sleep
    In still profounder rest.

THE COUNTESS

Throw back the locust's flowery plume,
    The birch's pale-green scarf,
And break the web of brier and bloom
    From name and epitaph.

A simple muster-roll of death,
    Of pomp and romance shorn,
The dry, old names that common breath
    Has cheapened and outworn.

Yet pause by one low mound, and part
    The wild vines o'er it laced,
And read the words by rustic art
    Upon its headstone traced.

Haply yon white-haired villager
    Of fourscore years can say
What means the noble name of her
    Who sleeps with common clay.

An exile from the Gascon land
    Found refuge here and rest,
And loved, of all the village band,
    Its fairest and its best.

He knelt with her on Sabbath morns,
    He worshipped through her eyes,
And on the pride that doubts and scorns
    Stole in her faith's surprise.

Her simple daily life he saw
    By homeliest duties tried,
In all things by an untaught law
    Of fitness justified.

For her his rank aside he laid;
    He took the hue and tone
Of lowly life and toil, and made
    Her simple ways his own.

Yet still, in gay and careless ease,
    To harvest-field or dance
He brought the gentle courtesies,
    The nameless grace of France.

And she who taught him love not less
    From him she loved in turn
Caught in her sweet unconsciousness
    What love is quick to learn.

Each grew to each in pleased accord,
    Nor knew the gazing town
If she looked upward to her lord
    Or he to her looked down.

How sweet, when summer's day was o'er
    His violin's mirth and wail,
The walk on pleasant Newbury's shore.
    The river's moonlit sail!

Ah! life is brief, though love be long;
    The altar and the bier,
The burial hymn and bridal song,
    Were both in one short year!

Her rest is quiet on the hill,
    Beneath the locust's bloom:
Far off her lover sleeps as still
    Within his scutcheoned tomb.

The Gascon lord, the village maid,
    In death still clasp their hands;
The love that levels rank and grade
    Unites their severed lands.

What matter whose the hillside grave,
    Or whose the blazoned stone?
Forever to her western wave
    Shall whisper blue Garonne!

O Love!—so hallowing every soil
    That gives thy sweet flower room,
Wherever, nursed by ease or toil,
    The human heart takes bloom!—

Plant of lost Eden, from the sod
    Of sinful earth unriven,
White blossom of the trees of God
    Dropped down to us from heaven!—

This tangled waste of mound and stone
    Is holy for thy sake;
A sweetness which is all thy own
    Breathes out from fern and brake.

And while ancestral pride shall twine
    The Gascon's tomb with flowers,
Fall sweetly here, O song of mine,
    With summer's bloom and showers!

And let the lines that severed seem
    Unite again in thee,
As western wave and Gallic stream
    Are mingled in one sea!

OUR STATE

The South-land boasts its teeming cane,
The prairied West its heavy grain,
And sunset's radiant gates unfold
On rising marts and sands of gold!

Rough, bleak, and hard, our little State
Is scant of soil, of limits strait;
Her yellow sands are sands alone,
Her only mines are ice and stone!

From Autumn frost to April rain,
Too long her winter woods complain;
From budding flower to falling leaf,
Her summer time is all too brief.

Yet, on her rocks, and on her sands,
And wintry hills, the school-house stands,
And what her rugged soil denies,
The harvest of the mind supplies.

The riches of the Commonwealth
Are free, strong minds, and hearts of health;
And more to her than gold or grain,
The cunning hand and cultured brain.

For well she keeps her ancient stock,
The stubborn strength of Pilgrim Rock;
And still maintains, with milder laws,
And clearer light, the Good Old Cause!

Nor needs the sceptic's puny hands,
While near her school the church-spire stands;
Nor fears the blinded bigot's rule,
While near her church-spire stands the school.

STANZAS

Afterwards entitled "Follen" and "Expostulation." Whittier's first published anti-slavery poem, printed in the Liberator on September 20th, 1834. Parliament had freed all of the 800,000 slaves in the British Dominions in 1833 and Whittier wrote this poem denouncing our enslaving of 2,500,000.

Our fellow-countrymen in chains!
    Slaves—in a land of light and law!
Slaves—crouching on the very plains
    Where rolled the storm of Freedom's war!
A groan from Eutaw's haunted wood,—
    A wail where Camden's martyrs fell,—
By every shrine of patriot blood,
    From Moultrie's wall and Jaspar's well!

By storied hill and hallowed grot,
    By mossy wood and marshy glen,
Whence rang of old the rifle-shot,
    And hurrying shout of Marion's men!
The groan of breaking hearts is there,—
    The falling lash,—the fetter's clank!
Slaves,—SLAVES are breathing in that air,
    Which old DeKalb and Sumter drank!

What, ho!—our countrymen in chains!
    The whip on WOMAN'S shrinking flesh!
Our soil yet reddening with the stains
    Caught from her scourging, warm and fresh!
What! mothers from their children riven!
    What! God's own image bought and sold!
AMERICANS to market driven,
    And bartered as the brute for gold!

Speak! shall their agony of prayer
    Come thrilling to our hearts in vain?
To us whose fathers scorned to bear
    The paltry menace of a chain;
To us, whose boast is loud and long
    Of holy Liberty and Light,—
Say, shall these writhing slaves of Wrong
    Plead vainly for their plundered Right?

What! shall we send, with lavish breath,
    Our sympathies across the wave,
Where Manhood, on the field of death,
    Strikes for his freedom or a grave?
Shall prayers go up, and hymns be sung
    For Greece, the Moslem fetter spurning,
And millions hail with pen and tongue
    Our light on all her altars burning?

Shall Belgium feel, and gallant France,
    By Vendome's pile and Schoenbrun's wall,
And Poland, gasping on her lance,
    The impulse of our cheering call?

And shall the SLAVE, beneath our eye,
    Clank o'er our fields his hateful chain?
And toss his fettered arms on high,
    And groan for Freedom's gift, in vain?

O, say, shall Prussia's banner be
    A refuge for the stricken slave?
And shall the Russian serf go free
    By Baikal's lake and Neva's wave?
And shall the wintry-bosomed Dane
    Relax the iron hand of pride,
And bid his bondmen cast the chain,
    From fettered soul and limb, aside?

Shall every flap of England's flag
    Proclaim that all around are free,
From "farthest Ind" to each blue crag
    That beetles o'er the Western Sea?
And shall we scoff at Europe's kings,
    When Freedom's fire is dim with us,
And round our country's altar clings
    The damning shade of Slavery's curse?

Go—let us ask of Constantine
    To loose his grasp on Poland's throat;
And beg the lord of Mahmoud's line
    To spare the struggling Suliote,—
Will not the scorching answer come
    From turbaned Turk, and scornful Russ:
"Go, loose your fettered slaves at home,
    Then turn, and ask the like of us!"

Just God! and shall we calmly rest,
    The Christian's scorn,—the heathen's mirth,—
Content to live the lingering jest
    And by-word of a mocking Earth?
Shall our own glorious land retain
    That curse which Europe scorns to bear?
Shall our own brethren drag the chain
    Which not even Russia's menials wear?

Up, then, in Freedom's manly part,
    From graybeard eld to fiery youth,
And on the nation's naked heart
    Scatter the living coals of Truth!
Up,—while ye slumber, deeper yet
    The shadow of our fame is growing!
Up,—while ye pause, our sun may set
    In blood, around our altars flowing!

Oh! rouse ye, ere the storm comes forth,—
    The gathered wrath of God and man,—
Like that which wasted Egypt's earth,
    When hail and fire above it ran.
Hear ye no warnings in the air?
    Feel ye no earthquake underneath?
Up,—up! why will ye slumber where
    The sleeper only wakes in death?

Up now for Freedom!—not in strife
    Like that your sterner fathers saw,—
The awful waste of human life,—
    The glory and the guilt of war:
But break the chain,—the yoke remove,
    And smite to earth Oppression's rod,
With those mild arms of Truth and Love,
    Made mighty through the living God!

Down let the shrine of Moloch sink,
    And leave no traces where it stood;
Nor longer let its idol drink
    His daily cup of human blood;
But rear another altar there,
    To Truth and Love and Mercy given,
And Freedom's gift, and Freedom's prayer,
    Shall call an answer down from Heaven!

SLAVE SHIPS

In April 1819, the French ship Le Rodeur *sailed from Bonny, Africa, for America with a crew of twenty-two and 160 negro slaves confined in the ship's hold. On approaching the equator, a terrible contagious malady broke out among the slaves that blinded them. It was aggravated by the scarcity of water, as each slave was allowed only two ounces of water a day, and by the extreme impurity of the air in the ship's hold where they were confined.*

Upon the advice of the ship's physician, the stricken slaves were brought on deck, from time to time, until some of them jumped overboard in the hope of being carried back to their home in Africa. The captain ordered several of the slaves shot and others hanged as an example to the rest. The disease attacked the crew and soon all but one was infected; he sailing the ship to port. Thirty-six of the blind slaves were thrown overboard as they were unsaleable. The Spanish slaver Leon *was sighted and help was asked but as all of the*

SLAVE SHIPS

members of its crew were blind from the same disease, it was drifting along without guidance and was never heard of afterwards. Le Rodeur *reached Guadaloupe on June 21, 1819, and within three days of reaching port the sole sailor unafflicted by the disease was attacked by the malady and lost his sight.*

"All ready?" cried the captain;
"Ay, ay!" the seamen said;
"Heave up the worthless lubbers,—
The dying and the dead."
Up from the slave-ship's prison
Fierce, bearded heads were thrust:
"Now let the sharks look to it,—
Toss up the dead ones first!"

Corpse after corpse came up,—
Death had been busy there;
Where every blow is mercy,
Why should the spoiler spare?
Corpse after corpse they cast
Sullenly from the ship,
Yet bloody with the traces
Of fetter-link and whip.

Gloomily stood the captain,
With his arms upon his breast,
With his cold brow sternly knotted,
And his iron lip compressed.
"Are all the dead dogs over?"
Growled through that matted lip,—
"The blind ones are no better,
Let's lighten the good ship."

Hark! from the ship's dark bosom,
The very sounds of hell!
The ringing clank of iron,—
The maniac's short, sharp yell!—
The hoarse, low curse, throat-stifled,—
The starving infant's moan,—
The horror of a breaking heart
Poured through a mother's groan.

Up from that loathsome prison
The stricken blind ones came:
Below, had all been darkness,—
Above, was still the same.
Yet the holy breath of heaven
Was sweetly breathing there,

And the heated brow of fever
  Cooled in the soft sea air.

"Overboard with them, shipmates!"
  Cutlass and dirk were plied;
Fettered and blind, one after one,
  Plunged down the vessel's side.
The sabre smote above,—
  Beneath, the lean shark lay,
Waiting with wide and bloody jaw
  His quick and human prey.

God of the earth! what cries
  Rang upward unto thee?
Voices of agony and blood,
  From ship-deck and from sea.
The last dull plunge was heard,—
  The last wave caught its stain,—
And the unsated shark looked up
  For human hearts in vain.

*   *   *   *   *

Red glowed the western waters,—
  The setting sun was there,
Scattering alike on wave and cloud
  His fiery mesh of hair.
Amidst a group in blindness,
  A solitary eye
Gazed, from the burdened slaver's deck,
  Into that burning sky.

"A storm," spoke out the gazer,
  "Is gathering and at hand,—
Curse on 't—I'd give my other eye
  For one firm rood of land."
And then he laughed,—but only
  His echoed laugh replied,—
For the blinded and the suffering
  Alone were at his side.

Night settled on the waters,
  And on a stormy heaven,
While fiercely on that lone ship's track
  The thunder-gust was driven.
"A sail!—thank God, a sail!"
  And as the helmsman spoke,
Up through the stormy murmur
  A shout of gladness broke.

SLAVE SHIPS

Down came the stranger vessel,
  Unheeding on her way,
So near that on the slaver's deck
  Fell off her driven spray.
"Ho! for the love of mercy,—
  We're perishing and blind!"
A wail of utter agony
  Came back upon the wind.

"Help us! for we are stricken
  With blindness every one;
Ten days we've floated fearfully,
  Unnoting star or sun.
Our ship's the slaver Leon,—
  We've but a score on board,—
Our slaves are all gone over,—
  Help,—for the love of God!"

On livid brows of agony
  The broad red lightning shone,—
But the roar of wind and thunder
  Stifled the answering groan;
Wailed from the broken waters
  A last despairing cry,
As, kindling in the stormy light,
  The stranger ship went by.

*   *   *   *   *

In the sunny Guadaloupe
  A dark-hulled vessel lay,—
With a crew who noted never
  The nightfall or the day.
The blossom of the orange
  Was white by every stream,
And tropic leaf, and flower, and bird
  Were in the warm sunbeam.

And the sky was bright as ever,
  And the moonlight slept as well,
On the palm-trees by the hillside,
  And the streamlet of the dell:
And the glances of the Creole
  Were still as archly deep,
And her smiles as full as ever
  Of passion and of sleep.

But vain were bird and blossom,
  The green earth and the sky,

And the smile of human faces,
   To the slaver's darkened eye;
At the breaking of the morning,
   At the star-lit evening time,
O'er a world of light and beauty
   Fell the blackness of his crime.

THE CHRISTIAN SLAVE

(In a late publication of L. F. Tasistro, Random Shots and Southern Breezes, *is a description of a slave auction at New Orleans, at which the auctioneer recommended the woman on the stand as "A Good Christian!")*

A CHRISTIAN! going, gone!
Who bids for God's own image?—for his grace,
Which that poor victim of the market-place
   Hath in her suffering won?

My God! can such things be?
Hast thou not said that whatsoe'er is done
Unto thy weakest and thy humblest one
   Is even done to thee?

In that sad victim, then,
Child of thy pitying love, I see thee stand,—
Once more the jest-word of a mocking band,
   Bound, sold, and scourged again!

A Christian up for sale!
Wet with her blood your whips, o'ertask her frame,
Make her life loathsome with your wrong and shame,
   Her patience shall not fail!

A heathen hand might deal
Back on your heads the gathered wrong of years:
But her low, broken prayer and nightly tears,
   Ye neither heed nor feel.

Con well thy lesson o'er,
Thou prudent teacher,—tell the toiling slave
No dangerous tale of Him who came to save
   The outcast and the poor.

But wisely shut the ray
Of God's free Gospel from her simple heart,
And to her darkened mind alone impart
   One stern command,—OBEY!

THE FAREWELL

    So shalt thou deftly raise
The market price of human flesh; and while
On thee, their pampered guest, the planters smile,
    Thy church shall praise.

    Grave, reverend men shall tell
From Northern pulpits how thy work was blest,
While in that vile South Sodom first and best,
    Thy poor disciples sell.

    O, shame! the Moslem thrall,
Who, with his master, to the Prophet kneels,
While turning to the sacred Kebla feels
    His fetters break and fall.

    Cheers for the turbaned Bey
Of robber-peopled Tunis! he hath torn
The dark slave-dungeons open, and hath borne
    Their inmates into day:

    But our poor slave in vain
Turns to the Christian shrine his aching eyes,—
Its rites will only swell his market price,
    And rivet on his chain.

    God of all right! how long
Shall priestly robbers at thine altar stand,
Lifting in prayer to thee, the bloody hand
    And haughty brow of wrong?

    O, from the fields of cane,
From the low rice-swamp, from the trader's cell,—
From the black slave-ship's foul and loathsome hell,
    And coffle's weary chain,—

    Hoarse, horrible, and strong,
Rises to Heaven that agonizing cry,
Filling the arches of the hollow sky,
    HOW LONG, O GOD, HOW LONG?

THE FAREWELL

The farewell of a Virginia Slave mother to her daughters sold into Southern bondage.

    Gone, gone,—sold and gone,
      To the rice-swamp dank and lone.
Where the slave-whip ceaseless swings,
Where the noisome insect stings,

THE FAREWELL

Where the fever demon strews
Poison with the falling dews,
Where the sickly sunbeams glare
Through the hot and misty air,—
    Gone? gone,—sold and gone,
    To the rice-swamp dank and lone.
    From Virginia's hills and waters,—
    Woe is me, my stolen daughters!

    Gone? gone,—sold and gone,
    To the rice-swamp dank and lone.
There no mother's eye is near them,
There no mother's ear can hear them;
Never, when the torturing lash
Seams their back with many a gash,
Shall a mother's kindness bless them,
Or a mother's arms caress them.
    Gone? gone,—sold and gone,
    To the rice-swamp dank and lone.
    From Virginia's hills and waters,—
    Woe is me, my stolen daughters!

    Gone? gone,—sold and gone,
    To the rice-swamp dank and lone.
O, when weary, sad, and slow,
From the fields at night they go,
Faint with toil, and racked with pain,
To their cheerless homes again,
There no brother's voice shall greet them,—
There no father's welcome meet them.
    Gone? gone,—sold and gone,
    To the rice-swamp dank and lone,
    From Virginia's hills and waters,—
    Woe is me, my stolen daughters!

    Gone? gone,—sold and gone,
    To the rice-swamp dank and lone,
From the tree whose shadow lay
On their childhood's place of play,—
From the cool spring where they drank,—
Rock, and hill, and rivulet bank,—
From the solemn house of prayer,
And the holy counsels there,—
    Gone? gone,—sold and gone,
    To the rice-swamp dank and lone,
    From Virginia's hills and waters,—
    Woe is me, my stolen daughters!

Gone? gone,—sold and gone,
  To the rice-swamp dank and lone,—
Toiling through the weary day,
And at night the spoiler's prey.
O that they had earlier died,
Sleeping calmly, side by side,
Where the tyrant's power is o'er,
And the fetter galls no more!
  Gone? gone,—sold and gone,
  To the rice-swamp dank and lone,
  From Virginia's hills and waters,—
  Woe is me, my stolen daughters!

Gone? gone,—sold and gone,
  To the rice-swamp dank and lone,
By the holy love He beareth,—
By the bruised reed He spareth,—
O, may He, to whom alone
All their cruel wrongs are known,
Still their hope and refuge prove,
With a more than mother's love.
  Gone? gone,—sold and gone,
  To the rice-swamp dank and lone,
  From Virginia's hills and waters,—
  Woe is me, my stolen daughters!

THE YANKEE GIRL

She sings by her wheel at that low cottage-door,
Which the long evening shadow is stretching before,
With a music as sweet as the music which seems
Breathed softly and faint in the ear of our dreams!

How brilliant and mirthful the light of her eye,
Like a star glancing out from the blue of the sky!
And lightly and freely her dark tresses play
O'er a brow and a bosom as lovely as they!

Who comes in his pride to that low cottage-door,—
The haughty and rich to the humble and poor?
'Tis the great Southern planter,—the master who waves
His whip of dominion o'er hundreds of slaves.

"Nay, Ellen,—for shame! Let those Yankee fools spin,
Who would pass for our slaves with a change of their skin;
Let them toil as they will at the loom or the wheel,
Too stupid for shame, and too vulgar to feel!

"But thou art too lovely and precious a gem
To be bound to their burdens and sullied by them,—
For shame, Ellen, shame,—cast thy bondage aside,
And away to the South, as my blessing and pride.

"O, come where no winter thy footsteps can wrong,
But where flowers are blossoming all the year long.
Where the shade of the palm-tree is over my home,
And the lemon and orange are white in their bloom!

"O, come to my home, where my servants shall all
Depart at thy bidding and come at thy call;
They shall heed thee as mistress with trembling and awe,
And each wish of thy heart shall be felt as a law."

O, could ye have seen her—that pride of our girl's—
Arise and cast back the dark wealth of her curls,
With a scorn in her eye which the gazer could feel,
And a glance like the sunshine that flashes on steel!

"Go back, haughty Southron! thy treasures of gold
Are dim with the blood of the hearts thou hast sold;
Thy home may be lovely, but round it I hear
The crack of the whip and the footsteps of fear!

"And the sky of thy South may be brighter than ours,
And greener thy landscapes, and fairer thy flowers;
But dearer the blast round our mountains which raves,
Than the sweet summer zephyr which breathes over slaves!

"Full low at thy bidding thy negroes may kneel,
With the iron of bondage on spirit and heel;
Yet know that the Yankee girl sooner would be
In fetters with them, than in freedom with thee!"

MASSACHUSETTS TO VIRGINIA

Whittier wrote this poem on reading an account of the proceedings of the citizens of Norfolk, Va., with reference to the arrest of George Latimer as a fugitive slave, and whom the Massachusetts Supreme Judicial Court, in 1836, denied the right to a trial by jury, holding that the Massachusetts law guaranteeing him such a right was unconstitutional. Latimer's freedom was bought for $400.00 by local anti-slavery leaders.

The blast from Freedom's Northern hills, upon its Southern way,
Bears greeting to Virginia from Massachusetts Bay:—
No word of haughty challenging, nor battle bugle's peal,
Nor sturdy tread of marching files, nor clang of horsemen's
    steel.

MASSACHUSETTS TO VIRGINIA

No trains of deep-mouthed cannon along our highways go,—
Around our silent arsenals untrodden lies the snow;
And to the land-breeze of our ports, upon their errands far,
A thousand sails of commerce swell, but none are spread for war.

We hear thy threats, Virginia! thy stormy words and high,
Swell harshly on the Southern winds which melt along our sky;
Yet, not one brown, hard hand foregoes its honest labor here,
No hewer of our mountain oaks suspends his axe in fear.

Wild are the waves which lash the reefs along St. George's bank,—
Cold on the shores of Labrador the fog lies white and dank;
Through storm, and wave, and blinding mist, stout are the hearts which man
The fishing-smacks of Marblehead, the sea-boats of Cape Ann.

The cold north light and wintry sun glare on their icy forms,
Bent grimly o'er their straining lines or wrestling with the storms;
Free as the winds they drive before, rough as the waves they roam,
They laugh to scorn the slaver's threat against their rocky home.

What means the Old Dominion? Hath she forgot the day
When o'er her conquered valleys swept the Briton's steel array?
How side by side, with sons of hers, the Massachusetts men
Encountered Tarleton's charge of fire, and stout Cornwallis, then?

Forgets she how the Bay State, in answer to the call
Of her old House of Burgesses, spoke out from Faneuil Hall?
When, echoing back her Henry's cry, came pulsing on each breath
Of Northern winds, the thrilling sounds of "LIBERTY or DEATH!"

What asks the Old Dominion? If now her sons have proved
False to their fathers' memory,—false to the faith they loved,
If she can scoff at Freedom, and its great charter spurn,
Must we of Massachusetts from truth and duty turn?

We hunt your bondmen, flying from Slavery's hateful hell,—
Our voices, at your bidding, take up the bloodhound's yell,—
We gather, at your summons, above our fathers' graves,
From Freedom's holy altar-horns to tear your wretched slaves!

Thank God! not yet so vilely can Massachusetts bow;
The spirit of her early time is with her even now;
Dream not because her Pilgrim blood moves slow and calm and cool,
She thus can stoop her chainless neck, a sister's slave and tool!

All that a sister State should do, all that a free State may,
Heart, hand, and purse we proffer, as in our early day;
But that one dark loathsome burden ye must stagger with alone,
And reap the bitter harvest which ye yourselves have sown!

Hold, while ye may, your struggling slaves, and burden God's free air
With woman's shriek beneath the lash, and manhood's wild despair;
Cling closer to the "cleaving curse" that writes upon your plains
The blasting of Almighty wrath against a land of chains.

Still shame your gallant ancestry, the cavaliers of old,
By watching round the shambles where human flesh is sold,—
Gloat o'er the new-born child, and count his market value, when
The maddened mother's cry of woe shall pierce the slaver's den!

Lower than plummet soundeth, sink the Virginia name;
Plant, if ye will, your fathers' graves with rankest weeds of shame;
Be, if ye will, the scandal of God's fair universe,—
We wash our hands forever of your sin and shame and curse.

A voice from lips whereon the coal from Freedom's shrine hath been,
Thrilled, as but yesterday, the hearts of Berkshire's mountain men:
The echoes of that solemn voice are sadly lingering still
In all our sunny valleys, on every wind-swept hill.

And when the prowling man-thief came hunting for his prey
Beneath the very shadow of Bunker's shaft of gray,
How, through the free lips of the son, the father's warning spoke;
How, from its bonds of trade and sect, the Pilgrim city broke!

A hundred thousand right arms were lifted up on high,—
A hundred thousand voices sent back their loud reply;
Through the thronged towns of Essex the startling summons rang,

And up from bench and loom and wheel her young mechanics
    sprang!

The voice of free, broad Middlesex,—of thousands as of one,—
The shaft of Bunker calling to that of Lexington,—
From Norfolk's ancient villages, from Plymouth's rocky bound
To where Nantucket feels the arms of ocean close her round;—

From rich and rural Worcester, where through the calm repose
Of cultured vales and fringing woods the gentle Nashua flows,
To where Wachuset's wintry blasts the mountain larches stir,
Swelled up to Heaven the thrilling cry of "God save Latimer!"

And sandy Barnstable rose up, wet with the salt sea spray,—
And Bristol sent her answering shout down Narragansett Bay!
Along the broad Connecticut Old Hampden felt the thrill,
And the cheer of Hampshire's woodmen swept down from
    Holyoke Hill.

The voice of Massachusetts! Of her free sons and daughters,—
Deep calling unto deep aloud,—the sound of many waters!
Against the burden of that voice what tyrant power shall
    stand?
No fetters in the Bay State! No slave upon her land!

Look to it well, Virginians! In calmness we have borne,
In answer to our faith and trust, your insult and your scorn;
You've spurned our kindest counsels,—you've hunted for our
    lives,—
And shaken round our hearths and homes your manacles and
    gyves!

We wage no war,—we lift no arm,—we fling no torch within
The fire-damps of the quaking mine beneath your soil of sin;
We leave ye with your bondmen, to wrestle while ye can,
With the strong upward tendencies and godlike soul of man!

But for us and for our children, the vow which we have given
For freedom and humanity is registered in heaven;
**No slave-hunt in our borders,—no pirate on our strand!
No fetters in the Bay State,—no slave upon our land!**

MOLOCH IN STATE STREET

*The bankers of State Street, Boston, put pressure on the
Boston police to allow the Federal officers to kidnap from them
the fugitive slave, Thomas Sims, and to return him to slavery.
Sims was removed at night by Federal officers while under*

MOLOCH IN STATE STREET

confinement in the court house and under arrest of the Boston police.

> The moon has set: while yet the dawn
>   Breaks cold and gray,
> Between the midnight and the morn
>   Bear off your prey!
>
> On, swift and still!—the conscious street
>   Is panged and stirred;
> Tread light!—that fall of serried feet
>   The dead have heard!
>
> The first drawn blood of Freedom's veins
>   Gushed where ye tread;
> Lo! through the dusk the martyr-stains
>   Blush darkly red!
>
> Beneath the slowly waning stars
>   And whitening day,
> What stern and awful presence bars
>   That sacred way?
>
> What faces frown upon ye, dark
>   With shame and pain?
> Come these from Plymouth's Pilgrim bark?
>   Is that young Vane?
>
> Who, dimly beckoning, speed ye on
>   With mocking cheer?
> Lo! spectral Andros, Hutchinson,
>   And Gage are here!
>
> For ready mart or favoring blast
>   Through Moloch's fire
> Flesh of his flesh, unsparing, passed
>   The Tyrian sire.
>
> Ye make that ancient sacrifice
>   Of Man to Gain,
> Your traffic thrives, where Freedom dies
>   Beneath the chain.
>
> Ye sow today, your harvest, scorn
>   And hate, is near;
> How think ye freemen, mountain-born,
>   The tale will hear?
>
> Thank God! our mother State can yet
>   Her fame retrieve;

To you and to your children let
    The scandal cleave.

Chain Hall and Pulpit, Court and Press,
    Make Gods of gold;
Let honor, truth, and manliness
    Like wares be sold.

Your hoards are great, your walls are strong,
    But God is just;
The gilded chambers built by wrong
    Invite the rust.

What! know ye not the gains of Crime
    Are dust and dross;
Its ventures on the waves of time
    Foredoomed to loss!

And still the Pilgrim State remains
    What she hath been;
Her inland hills, her seaward plains,
    Still nurture men!

Nor wholly lost the fallen mart,—
    Her olden blood
Through many a free and generous heart
    Still pours its flood.

That brave old blood, quick-flowing yet,
    Shall know no check,
Till a free people's foot is set
    On Slavery's neck.

Even now, the peal of bell and gun,
    And hills aflame,
Tell of the first great triumph won
    In freedom's name.

The long night dies: the welcome gray
    Of dawn we see;
Speed up the heavens thy perfect day,
    God of the free!

A SABBATH SCENE

Scarce had the solemn Sabbath-bell
    Ceased quivering in the steeple,
Scarce had the parson to his desk
    Walked stately through his people,

A SABBATH SCENE

When down the summer-shaded street
　　A wasted female figure,
With dusky brow and naked feet,
　　Came rushing wild and eager.

She saw the white spire through the trees,
　　She heard the sweet hymn swelling:
O pitying Christ! a refuge give
　　That poor one in thy dwelling!

Like a scared fawn before the hounds,
　　Right up the aisle she glided,
While close behind her, whip in hand,
　　A lank-haired hunter strided.

She raised a keen and bitter cry,
　　To Heaven and Earth appealing;—
Were manhood's generous pulses dead?
　　Had woman's heart no feeling?

A score of stout hands rose between
　　The hunter and the flying:
Age clenched his staff, and maiden eyes
　　Flashed tearful, yet defying.

"Who dares profane this house and day?"
　　Cried out the angry pastor.
"Why, bless your soul, the wench 's a slave,
　　And I'm her lord and master!

"I've law and gospel on my side,
　　And who shall dare refuse me?"
Down came the parson, bowing low,
　　"My good sir, pray excuse me!

"Of course I know your right divine
　　To own and work and whip her;
Quick, deacon, throw that Polyglott
　　Before the wench, and trip her!"

Plump dropped the holy tome, and o'er
　　Its sacred pages stumbling,
Bound hand and foot, a slave once more,
　　The hapless wretch lay trembling.

I saw the parson tie the knots,
　　The while his flock addressing,
The Scriptural claims of slavery
　　With text on text impressing.

A SABBATH SCENE

"Although," said he, "on Sabbath day
    All secular occupations
Are deadly sins, we must fulfill
    Our moral obligations:

"And this commends itself as one
    To every conscience tender;
As Paul sent back Onesimus,
    My Christian friends, we send her!"

Shriek rose on shriek,—the Sabbath air
    Her wild cries tore asunder;
I listened, with hushed breath, to hear
    God answering with his thunder!

All still!—the very altar's cloth
    Had smothered down her shrieking,
And, dumb, she turned from face to face,
    For human pity seeking!

I saw her dragged along the aisle,
    Her shackles harshly clanking;
I heard the parson, over all,
    The Lord devoutly thanking!

My brain took fire: "Is this," I cried,
    "The end of prayer and preaching?
Then down with pulpit, down with priest,
    And give us Nature's teaching!

"Foul shame and scorn be on ye all
    Who turn the good to evil,
And steal the Bible from the Lord,
    To give it to the Devil!

"Than garbled text or parchment law
    I own a statute higher;
And God is true, though every book
    And every man's a liar!"

Just then I felt the deacon's hand
    In wrath my coat-tail seize on;
I heard the priest cry, "Infidel!"
    The lawyer mutter, "Treason!"

I started up,—where now were church,
    Slave, master, priest, and people?
I only heard the supper-bell,
    Instead of clanging steeple.

But on the open window's sill,
   O'er which the white blooms drifted,
The pages of a good old Book
   The wind of summer lifted,

And flower and vine, like angel wings
   Around the Holy Mother,
Waved softly there, as if God's truth
   And Mercy kissed each other.

And freely from the cherry-bough
   Above the casement swinging,
With golden bosom to the sun,
   The oriole was singing.

As bird and flower made plain of old
   The lesson of the Teacher,
So now I heard the written Word
   Interpreted by Nature!

For to my ear methought the breeze
   Bore Freedom's blessed word on;
THUS SAITH THE LORD: BREAK EVERY YOKE,
   UNDO THE HEAVY BURDEN!

ICHABOD

Daniel Webster made a speech on March 7, 1850, in the United States Senate in which he demanded that the North make concessions to the South on the slavery issue in order to hold the South in the Union; Whittier considered that Webster had betrayed his constituents and wrote Ichabod as an answer to Webster's demand.

So fallen! so lost! the light withdrawn
   Which once he wore!
The glory from his gray hairs gone
   Forevermore!

Revile him not,—the Tempter hath
   A snare for all;
And pitying tears, not scorn and wrath,
   Befit his fall!

O, dumb be passion's stormy rage,
   When he who might
Have lighted up and led his age,
   Falls back in night.

Scorn! would the angels laugh, to mark
    A bright soul driven,
Fiend-goaded, down the endless dark,
    From hope and heaven!

Let not the land once proud of him
    Insult him now,
Nor brand with deeper shame his dim,
    Dishonored brow.

But let its humbled sons, instead,
    From sea to lake,
A long lament, as for the dead,
    In sadness make.

Of all we loved and honored, naught
    Save power remains,—
A fallen angel's pride of thought,
    Still strong in chains.

All else is gone, from those great eyes
    The soul has fled;
When faith is lost, when honor dies,
    The man is dead!

Then, pay the reverence of old days
    To his dead fame;
Walk backward, with averted gaze,
    And hide the shame!

THE KANSAS EMIGRANTS

A marching song of the Northerners as they rushed in to settle Kansas as free soil. It was sung to the tune of "Auld Lang Syne." Published in 1854.

We cross the prairie as of old
    The Pilgrims crossed the sea,
To make the West, as they the East,
    The homestead of the free!

We go to rear a wall of men
    On Freedom's Southern line,
And plant beside the cotton-tree
    The rugged Northern pine!

We're flowing from our native hills
    As our free rivers flow;
The blessing of our Mother-land
    Is on us as we go.

We go to plant her common schools
    On distant prairie swells,
And give the Sabbaths of the wild
    The music of her bells.

Upbearing, like the Ark of old,
    The Bible in our van,
We go to test the truth of God
    Against the fraud of man.

No pause, nor rest, save where the streams
    That feed the Kansas run,
Save where our Pilgrim gonfalon
    Shall flout the setting sun!

We'll tread the prairie as of old
    Our fathers sailed the sea,
And make the West, as they the East,
    The homestead of the free!

THE PRISONER FOR DEBT
1835

Look on him!—through his dungeon grate
    Feebly and cold, the morning light
Comes stealing round him, dim and late,
    As if it loathed the sight.
Reclining on his strawy bed,
His hand upholds his drooping head,—
His bloodless cheek is seamed and hard,
Unshorn his gray, neglected beard;
And o'er his bony fingers flow
His long, dishevelled locks of snow.

No grateful fire before him glows,
    And yet the winter's breath is chill,
And o'er his half-clad person goes
    The frequent ague thrill!
Silent, save ever and anon,
A sound, half murmur and half groan,
Forces apart the painful grip
Of the old sufferer's bearded lip;
Oh, sad and crushing is the fate
Of old age chained and desolate!

Just God! why lies that old man there?
    A murderer shares his prison bed,
Whose eyeballs, through his horrid hair,
    Gleam on him, fierce and red;

THE PRISONER FOR DEBT

And the rude oath and heartless jeer
Fall ever on his loathing ear,
And, or in wakefulness or sleep,
Nerve, flesh, and pulses thrill and creep
Whene'er that ruffian's tossing limb,
Crimson with murder, touches him!

What has the gray-haired prisoner done?
    Has murder stained his hands with gore?
Not so; his crime's a fouler one;
    GOD MADE THE OLD MAN POOR!
For this he shares a felon's cell,
The fittest earthly type of hell!
For this, the boon for which he poured
His young blood on the invader's sword,
And counted light the fearful cost,—
His blood-gained liberty is lost!

And so, for such a place of rest,
    Old prisoner, dropped thy blood as rain
On Concord's field, and Bunker's crest,
    And Saratoga's plain?
Look forth, thou man of many scars,
Through thy dim dungeon's iron bars;
It must be joy, in sooth, to see
Yon monument upreared to thee,—
Piled granite and a prison cell,—
The land repays thy service well!

Go, ring the bells and fire the guns,
    And fling the starry banner out;
Shout "Freedom!" till your lisping ones
    Give back their cradle-shout;
Let boastful eloquence declaim
Of honor, liberty, and fame;
Still let the poet's strain be heard,
With glory for each second word,
And everything with breath agree
To praise "our glorious liberty!"

But, when the patron cannon jars
    That prison's cold and gloomy wall,
And through its grates the stripes and stars
    Rise on the wind, and fall,—
Think ye that prisoner's aged ear
Rejoices in the general cheer?
Think ye his dim and failing eye
Is kindled at your pageantry?

Sorrowing of soul, and chained of limb,
What is your carnival to him?

Down with the LAW that binds him thus!
    Unworthy freemen, let it find
No refuge from the withering curse
    Of God and human kind!
Open the prison's living tomb,
And usher from its brooding gloom
The victims of your savage code
To the free sun and air of God;
No longer dare as crime to brand
The chastening of the Almighty's hand.

THE POOR VOTER ON ELECTION DAY

The proudest now is but my peer,
    The highest not more high;
To-day, of all the weary year,
    A king of men am I.
To-day, alike are great and small,
    The nameless and the known;
My palace is the people's hall,
    The ballot-box my throne!

Who serves to-day upon the list
    Beside the served shall stand;
Alike the brown and wrinkled fist,
    The gloved and dainty hand!
The rich is level with the poor,
    The weak is strong to-day;
And sleekest broadcloth counts no more
    Than homespun frock of gray.

To-day let pomp and vain pretence
    My stubborn right abide;
I set a plain man's common sense
    Against the pedant's pride.
To-day shall simple manhood try
    The strength of gold and land;
The wide world has not wealth to buy
    The power in my right hand!

While there's a grief to seek redress,
    Or balance to adjust,
Where weighs our living manhood less
    Than Mammon's vilest dust,—
While there's a right to need my vote,
    A wrong to sweep away,
Up! clouted knee and ragged coat!
    A man's a man to-day!

PENTUCKET 1708

This poem deals with the French and Indian attack on Haverhill August 29, 1708. The defeat of the French convinced them that it was useless to try to drive the English out of New England.

How sweetly on the wood-girt town
The mellow light of sunset shone!
Each small, bright lake, whose waters still
Mirror the forest and the hill,
Reflected from its waveless breast
The beauty of a cloudless west,
Glorious as if a glimpse were given
Within the western gates of heaven,
Left, by the spirit of the star
Of sunset's holy hour, ajar!

Beside the river's tranquil flood
The dark and low-walled dwellings stood,
Where many a rood of open land
Stretched up and down on either hand,
With corn-leaves waving freshly green
The thick and blackened stumps between.
Behind, unbroken, deep and dread,
The wild, untravelled forest spread,
Back to those mountains, white and cold,
Of which the Indian trapper told,
Upon whose summits never get
Was mortal foot in safety set.

Quiet and calm, without a fear
Of danger darkly lurking near,
The weary laborer left his plough,—
The milkmaid carolled by her cow,—
From cottage door and household hearth
Rose songs of praise, or tones of mirth.
At length the murmur died away,
And silence on that village lay,—
So slept Pompeii, tower and hall,
Ere the quick earthquake swallowed all,
Undreaming of the fiery fate
Which made its dwellings desolate!

Hours passed away. By moonlight sped
The Merrimack along his bed.
Bathed in the pallid lustre, stood
Dark cottage-wall and rock and wood,
Silent, beneath that tranquil beam,

As the hushed grouping of a dream.
Yet on the still air crept a sound,—
No bark of fox, nor rabbit's bound,
Nor stir of wings, nor waters flowing,
Nor leaves in midnight breezes blowing.

Was that the tread of many feet,
Which downward from the hillside beat?
What forms were those which darkly stood
Just on the margin of the wood?—
Charred tree-stumps in the moonlight dim,
Or paling rude, or leafless limb?
No,—through the trees fierce eyeballs glowed,
Dark human forms in moonshine showed,
Wild from their native wilderness,
With painted limbs and battle-dress!

A yell the dead might wake to hear
Swelled on the night air, far and clear,—
Then smote the Indian tomahawk
On crashing door and shattering lock,—
Then rang the rifle-shot,—and then
The shrill death-scream of stricken men,—
Sank the red axe in woman's brain,
And childhood's cry arose in vain,—
Bursting through roof and window came,
Red, fast, and fierce, the kindled flame;
And blended fire and moonlight glared
On still dead men and weapons bared.

The morning sun looked brightly through
The river willows, wet with dew.
No sound of combat filled the air,—
No shout was heard,—nor gunshot there;
Yet still the thick and sullen smoke
From smouldering ruins slowly broke;
And on the greensward many a stain,
And, here and there, the mangled slain,
Told how that midnight bolt had sped
Pentucket, on thy fated head!

Even now the villager can tell
Where Rolfe beside his hearthstone fell,
Still show the door of wasting oak,
Through which the fatal death-shot broke,
And point the curious stranger where
DeRouville's corpse lay grim and bare,—
Whose hideous head, in death still feared,
Bore not a trace of hair or beard,—

And still, within the churchyard ground,
Heaves darkly up the ancient mound,
Whose grass-grown surface overlies
The victims of that sacrifice.

THE MERRIMACK

"The Indians speak of a beautiful river, far to the south, which they call Merrimack."—Sieur de Monts, 1604.

Stream of my fathers! sweetly still
The sunset rays thy valley fill;
Poured slantwise down the long defile,
Wave, wood, and spire beneath them smile.
I see the winding Powow fold
The green hill in its belt of gold,
And following down its wavy line,
Its sparkling waters blend with thine.
There's not a tree upon thy side,
Nor rock, which thy returning tide
As yet hath left abrupt and stark
Above thy evening water-mark;
No calm cove with its rocky hem,
No isle whose emerald swells begem
Thy broad, smooth current; not a sail
Bowed to the freshening ocean gale;
No small boat with its busy oars,
Nor gray wall sloping to thy shores;
Nor farm-house with its maple shade,
Or rigid poplar colonnade,
But lies distinct and full in sight,
Beneath this gush of sunset light.
Centuries ago, that harbor-bar,
Stretching its length of foam afar,
And Salisbury's beach of shining sand,
And yonder island's wave-smoothed strand,
Saw the adventurer's tiny sail,
Flit, stooping from the eastern gale;
And o'er these woods and waters broke
The cheer from Britain's hearts of oak,
As brightly on the voyager's eye,
Weary of forest, sea, and sky,
Breaking the dull continuous wood,
The Merrimack rolled down his flood;
Mingling that clear pellucid brook,
Which channels vast Agioochook
When spring-time's sun and shower unlock
The frozen fountains of the rock,
And more abundant waters given

From that pure lake, "The Smile of Heaven,"
Tributes from vale and mountain side,—
With ocean's dark, eternal tide!

On yonder rocky cape, which braves
The stormy challenge of the waves,
Midst tangled vine and dwarfish wood,
The hardy Anglo-Saxon stood,
Planting upon the topmost crag
The staff of England's battle-flag;
And, while from out its heavy fold
Saint George's crimson cross unrolled,
Midst roll of drum and trumpet blare,
And weapons brandishing in air,
He gave to that lone promontory
The sweetest name in all his story;
Of her, the flower of Islam's daughters,
Whose harems look on Stamboul's waters,—
Who, when the chance of war had bound
The Moslem chain his limbs around,
Wreathed o'er with silk that iron chain,
Soothed with her smiles his hours of pain,
And fondly to her youthful slave
A dearer gift than freedom gave.

But look!—the yellow light no more
Streams down on wave and verdant shore;
And clearly on the calm air swells
The twilight voice of distant bells.
From Ocean's bosom, white and thin,
The mists come slowly rolling in;
Hills, woods, the river's rocky rim,
Amidst the sea-like vapor swim,
While yonder lonely coast-light, set
Within its wave-washed minaret,
Half quenched, a beamless star and pale,
Shines dimly through its cloudy veil!
Home of my fathers!—I have stood
Where Hudson rolled his lordly flood;
Seen sunrise rest and sunset fade
Along his frowning Palisade;
Looked down the Apalachian peak
On Juniata's silver streak;
Have seen along his valley gleam
The Mohawk's softly winding stream;
The level light of sunset shine
Through broad Potomac's hem of pine;
And autumn's rainbow-tinted banner

THE SYCAMORES

Hang lightly o'er the Susquehanna;
Yet wheresoe'er his step might be,
Thy wandering child looked back to thee!
Heard in his dreams thy river's sound
Of murmuring on its pebbly bound,
The unforgotten swell and roar
Of waves on thy familiar shore;
And saw, amidst the curtained gloom
And quiet of his lonely room,
Thy sunset scenes before him pass;
As, in Agrippa's magic glass,
The loved and lost arose to view,
Remembered groves in greenness grew,
Bathed still in childhood's morning dew,
Along whose bowers of beauty swept
Whatever Memory's mourners wept,
Sweet faces, which the charnel kept,
Young, gentle eyes, which long had slept;
And while the gazer leaned to trace,
More near, some dear familiar face,
He wept to find the vision flown,—
A phantom and a dream alone!

THE SYCAMORES

This poem was written in memory of Hugh Tallant, the first Irishman in Haverhill, who planted the sycamores, or buttonwoods, in 1738, in front of Mr. Saltonstall's (his employer's) house on Water Street in Haverhill, the present site of the Haverhill Historical Society. One of the buttonwood trees still stands and the district is known locally as the "Buttonwood District." Mr. Tallant had a local reputation as a fiddler for dances. Written 1857.

In the outskirts of the village,
 On the river's winding shores,
Stand the Occidental plane-trees,
 Stand the ancient sycamores.

One long century hath been numbered,
 And another half-way told,
Since the rustic Irish gleeman
 Broke for them the virgin mould.

Deftly set to Celtic music,
 At his violin's sound they grew,
Through the moonlit eves of summer,
 Making Amphion's fable true.

Rise again, thou poor Hugh Tallant!
  Pass in jerkin green along,
With thy eyes brimful of laughter,
  And thy mouth as full of song.

Pioneer of Erin's outcasts,
  With his fiddle and his pack;
Little dreamed the village Saxons
  Of the myriads at his back.

How he wrought with spade and fiddle,
  Delved by day and sang by night,
With a hand that never wearied,
  And a heart forever light,—

Still the gay tradition mingles
  With a record grave and drear,
Like the rolic air of Cluny,
  With the solemn march of Mear.

When the box-tree, white with blossoms,
  Made the sweet May woodlands glad,
And the Aronia by the river
  Lighted up the swarming shad,

And the bulging nets swept shoreward,
  With their silver-sided haul,
Midst the shouts of dripping fishers,
  He was merriest of them all.

When, among the jovial huskers,
  Love stole in at Labor's side
With the lusty airs of England,
  Soft his Celtic measures vied.

Songs of love and wailing lyke-wake,
  And the merry fair's carouse;
Of the wild Red Fox of Erin
  And the Woman of Three Cows,

By the blazing hearths of winter,
  Pleasant seemed his simple tales,
Midst the grimmer Yorkshire legends
  And the mountain myths of Wales.

How the souls in Purgatory
  Scrambled up from fate forlorn,
On St. Keven's sackcloth ladder,
  Slyly hitched to Satan's horn.

THE SYCAMORES

Of the fiddler who at Tara
   Played all night to ghosts of kings;
Of the brown dwarfs, and the fairies
   Dancing in their moorland rings!

Jolliest of our birds of singing,
   Best he loved the Bob-o-link.
"Hush!" he'd say, "the tipsy fairies!
   Hear the little folks in drink!"

Merry-faced, with spade and fiddle,
   Singing through the ancient town,
Only this, of poor Hugh Tallant,
   Hath Tradition handed down.

Not a stone his grave discloses;
   But if yet his spirit walks,
'Tis beneath the trees he planted,
   And when Bob-o-Lincoln talks;

Green memorials of the gleeman!
   Linking still the river-shores,
With their shadows cast by sunset,
   Stand Hugh Tallant's sycamores!

When the Father of his Country
   Through the north-land riding came,
And the roofs were starred with banners,
   And the steeples rang acclaim,—

When each war-scarred Continental,
   Leaving smithy, mill, and farm,
Waved his rusted sword in welcome,
   And shot off his old king's-arm,—

Slowly passed that august Presence
   Down the thronged and shouting street;
Village girls as white as angels,
   Scattering flowers around his feet.

Midway, where the plane-tree's shadow
   Deepest fell, his rein he drew:
On his stately head, uncovered,
   Cool and soft the west-wind blew.

And he stood up in his stirrups,
   Looking up and looking down
On the hills of Gold and Silver
   Rimming round the little town,—

On the river, full of sunshine,
  To the lap of greenest vales
Winding down from wooded headlands,
  Willow-skirted, white with sails.

And he said, the landscape sweeping
  Slowly with his ungloved hand,
"I have seen no prospect fairer
  In this goodly Eastern land."

Then the bugles of his escort
  Stirred to life the cavalcade:
And that head, so bare and stately,
  Vanished down the depths of shade.

Ever since, in town and farm-house,
  Life has had its ebb and flow;
Thrice hath passed the human harvest
  To its garner green and low.

But the trees the gleeman planted,
  Through the changes, changeless stand;
As the marble calm of Tadmor
  Marks the desert's shifting sand.

Still the level moon at rising
  Silvers o'er each stately shaft;
Still beneath them, half in shadow,
  Singing, glides the pleasure craft.

Still beneath them, arm-enfolded,
  Love and Youth together stray;
While, as heart to heart beats faster,
  More and more their feet delay.

Where the ancient cobbler, Keezar,
  On the open hillside wrought,
Singing, as he drew his stitches,
  Songs his German masters taught.

Singing, with his gray hair floating
  Round his rosy ample face,—
Now a thousand Saxon craftsmen
  Stitch and hammer in his place.

All the pastoral lanes so grassy
  Now are Traffic's dusty streets;
From the village, grown a city,
  Fast the rural grace retreats.

But, still green, and tall, and stately,
    On the river's winding shores,
Stand the Occidental plane-trees,
    Stand Hugh Tallant's sycamores.

THE SHOEMAKERS

Ho! workers of the old time styled
    The Gentle Craft of Leather!
Young brothers of the ancient guild,
    Stand forth once more together!
Call out again your long array,
    In the olden merry manner!
Once more, on gay St. Crispin's day,
    Fling out your blazoned banner!

Rap, rap! upon the well worn stone
    How falls the polished hammer!
Rap, rap! the measured sound has grown
    A quick and merry clamor.
Now shape the sole! now deftly curl
    The glossy vamp around it,
And bless the while the bright-eyed girl
    Whose gentle fingers bound it!

For you, along the Spanish main
    A hundred keels are ploughing;
For you, the Indian on the plain
    His lasso-coil is throwing;
For you, deep glens with hemlock dark
    The woodman's fire is lighting;
For you, upon the oak's gray bark,
    The woodman's axe is smiting.

For you, from Carolina's pine
    The rosin-gum is stealing;
For you, the dark-eyed Florentine
    Her silken skein is reeling;
For you, the dizzy goatherd roams
    His rugged Alpine ledges;
For you, round all her shepherd homes
    Bloom England's thorny hedges.

The foremost still, by day or night,
    On moated mound or heather,
Where'er the need of trampled right
    Brought toiling men together;
Where the free burghers from the wall
    Defied the mail-clad master,

Than yours, at Freedom's trumpet-call,
　　No craftsmen rallied faster.

Let foplings sneer, let fools deride,—
　　Ye heed no idle scorner;
Free hands and hearts are still your pride,
　　And duty done, your honor.
Ye dare to trust, for honest fame,
　　The jury Time empanels,
And leave to truth each noble name
　　Which glorifies your annals.

Thy songs, Han Sachs, are living yet,
　　In strong and hearty German;
And Bloomfield's lay, and Gifford's wit,
　　And patriot fame of Sherman;
Still from his book, a mystic seer,
　　The soul of Behmen teaches,
And England's priestcraft shakes to hear
　　Of Fox's leathern breeches.

The foot is yours; where'er it falls,
　　It treads your well-wrought leather,
On earthen floor, in marble halls,
　　On carpet, or on heather.
Still there the sweetest charm is found
　　Of matron grace or vestal's
As Hebe's foot bore nectar round
　　Among the old celestials!

Rap rap!—your stout and bluff brogan,
　　With footsteps slow and weary,
May wander where the sky's blue span
　　Shuts down upon the prairie.
On Beauty's foot your slippers glance,
　　By Saratoga's fountains,
Or twinkle down the summer dance
　　Beneath the Crystal Mountains!

The red brick to the mason's hand,
　　The brown earth to the tiller's,
The shoe in yours shall wealth command,
　　Like fairy Cinderella's!
As they who shunned the household maid
　　Beheld the crown upon her,
So all shall see your toil repaid
　　With hearth and home and honor.

> Then let the toast be freely quaffed,
> In water cool and brimming,—
> "All honor to the good old Craft,
> Its merry men and women!"
> Call out again your long array,
> In the old time's pleasant manner:
> Once more, on gay St. Crispin's day,
> Fling out his blazoned banner!

THE HUSKERS

It was late in mild October, and the long autumnal rain
Had left the summer harvest-fields all green with grass again;
The first sharp frosts had fallen, leaving all the woodlands gay
With the hues of summer's rainbow, or the meadow-flowers of May.

Through a thin, dry mist, that morning, the sun rose broad and red,
At first a rayless disk of fire, he brightened as he sped;
Yet, even his noontide glory fell chastened and subdued,
On the cornfields and the orchards, and softly pictured wood.

And all that quiet afternoon, slow sloping to the night,
He wove with golden shuttle the haze with yellow light;
Slanting through the painted beeches, he glorified the hill;
And, beneath it, pond and meadow lay brighter, greener still.

And shouting boys in woodland haunts caught glimpses of that sky,
Flecked by the many-tinted leaves, and laughed, they knew not why;
And school-girls, gay with aster-flowers, beside the meadow brooks,
Mingled the glow of autumn with the sunshine of sweet looks.

From spire and barn looked westerly the patient weathercocks;
But even the birches on the hill stood motionless as rocks.
No sound was in the woodlands, save the squirrel's dropping shell,
And the yellow leaves among the boughs, low rustling as they fell.

The summer grains were harvested; the stubble-fields lay dry,
Where June winds rolled, in light and shade, the pale green waves of rye;
But still, on gentle hill-slopes, in valleys fringed with wood,
Ungathered, bleaching in the sun, the heavy corn crop stood.

THE CORN SONG

Bent low, by autumn's wind and rain, through husks that, dry and sere,
Unfolded from their ripened charge, shone out the yellow ear;
Beneath, the turnip lay concealed, in many a verdant fold,
And glistened in the slanting light the pumpkin's sphere of gold.

There wrought the busy harvesters; and many a creaking wain
Bore slowly to the long barn-floor its load of husk and grain;
Till broad and red, as when he rose, the sun sank down, at last,
And like a merry guest's farewell, the day in brightness passed.

And lo! as through the western pines, on meadow, stream, and pond,
Flamed the red radiance of a sky, set all afire beyond,
Slowly o'er the eastern sea-buffs a milder glory shone,
And the sunset and the moonrise were mingled into one!

As thus into the quiet night the twilight lapsed away,
And deeper in the brightening moon the tranquil shadows lay;
From many a brown old farm-house, and hamlet without name,
Their milking and their home-tasks done, the merry huskers came.

Swung o'er the heaped-up harvest, from pitchforks in the mow,
Shone dimly down the lanterns on the pleasant scene below;
The growing pile of husks behind, the golden ears before,
And laughing eyes and busy hands and brown cheeks glimmering o'er.

Half hidden in a quiet nook, serene of look and heart,
Talking their old times over, the old men sat apart;
While, up and down the unhusked pile, or nestling in its shade,
At hide-and-seek, with laugh and shout, the happy children played.

Urged by the good host's daughter, a maiden young and fair,
Lifting to light her sweet blue eyes and pride of soft brown hair,
The master of the village school, sleek of hair and smooth of tongue,
To the quaint tune of some old psalm, a husking-ballad sung.

THE CORN SONG

Heap high the farmer's wintry hoard!
Heap high the golden corn!
No richer gift has Autumn poured
From out her lavish horn!

THE CORN SONG

Let other lands, exulting, glean
    The apple from the pine,
The orange from its glossy green,
    The cluster from the vine;

We better love the hardy gift
    Our rugged vales bestow,
To cheer us when the storm shall drift
    Our harvest-fields with snow.

Through vales of grass and meads of flowers
    Our ploughs their furrows made,
While on the hills the sun and showers
    Of changeful April played.

We dropped the seed o'er hill and plain,
    Beneath the sun of May,
And frightened from our sprouting grain
    The robber crows away.

All through the long, bright days of June
    Its leaves grew green and fair,
And waved in hot midsummer's moon
    Its soft and yellow hair.

And now, with autumn's moonlit eves,
    Its harvest-time has come,
We pluck away the frosted leaves,
    And bear the treasure home.

There, richer than the fabled gift
    Apollo showered of old,
Fair hands the broken grain shall sift,
    And knead its meal of gold.

Let vapid idlers loll in silk
    Around their costly board;
Give us the bowl of samp and milk,
    By homespun beauty poured!

Where'er the wide old kitchen hearth
    Sends up its smoky curls,
Who will not thank the kindly earth,
    And bless our farmer girls!

Then shame on all the proud and vain,
    Whose folly laughs to scorn
The blessing of our hardy grain,
    Our wealth of golden corn!

Let earth withhold her goodly root,
    Let mildew blight the rye,
Give to the worm the orchard's fruit,
    The wheat-field to the fly:

But let the good old crop adorn
    The hills our fathers trod;
Still let us, for his golden corn,
    Send up our thanks to God!

TELLING THE BEES

This was one of Whittier's favorite poems. It is based on an old custom brought to New England from Europe requiring that the bees be informed of a death in the family. The hives were dressed in mourning to prevent them from swarming to a new home.

Here is the place, right over the hill
    Runs the path I took;
You can see the gap in the old wall still,
    And the stepping-stones in the shallow brook.

There is the house, with the gate red-barred,
    And the poplars tall;
And the barn's brown length, and the cattle-yard,
    And the white horns tossing above the wall.

There are the beehives ranged in the sun;
    And down by the brink
Of the brook are her poor flowers, weed-o'errun,
    Pansy and daffodil, rose and pink.

A year has gone, as the tortoise goes,
    Heavy and slow;
And the same rose blows, and the same gun glows,
    And the same brook sings of a year ago.

There's the same sweet clover-smell in the breeze;
    And the June sun warm
Tangles his wings of fire in the trees,
    Setting, as then, over Fernside farm.

I mind me how with a lover's care
    From my Sunday coat
I brushed off the burrs, and smoothed my hair,
    And cooled at the brookside my brow and throat.

Since we parted, a month had passed,—
  To love, a year;
Down through the beeches I looked at last
  On the little red gate and the well-sweep near.

I can see it all now,—the slantwise rain
  Of light through the leaves,
The sundown's blaze on her window-pane,
  The bloom of her roses under the eaves.

Just the same as a month before,—
  The house and the trees,
The barn's brown gable, the vine by the door,—
  Nothing changed but the hives of bees.

Before them, under the garden wall,
  Forward and back,
Went drearily singing the chore-girl small,
  Draping each hive with a shred of black.

Trembling, I listened: the summer sun
  Had the chill of snow;
For I knew she was telling the bees of one
  Gone on the journey we all must go!

Then I said to myself, "My Mary weeps
  For the dead today:
Haply her blind old grandsire sleeps
  The fret and the pain of his age away."

But her dog whined low; on the door-way sill,
  With his cane to his chin,
The old man sat; and the chore-girl still
  Sung to the bees stealing out and in.

And the song she was singing ever since
  In my ear sounds on:—
"Stay at home, pretty bees, fly not hence!
  Mistress Mary is dead and gone!"

THE CAPTAIN'S WELL

Captain Valentine Bagley, of Amesbury, Mass., was shipwrecked off the coast of Arabia. He suffered so of thirst on the desert that he vowed he would dig a well of pure water for all to drink, if he ever reached Amesbury again. He arrived home and dug the well in the place as he had vowed. It is still in use in front of the Amesbury High School but the water is supplied from the town's water main.

THE CAPTAIN'S WELL

From pain and peril, by land and main,
The shipwrecked sailor came back again;

And like one from the dead, the threshold cross'd
Of his wondering home, that had mourned him lost,

Where he sat once more with his kith and kin,
And welcomed his neighbors thronging in.

But when morning came he called for his spade,
"I must pay my debt to the Lord," he said.

"Why dig you here?" asked the passer-by;
"Is there gold or silver the road so nigh?"

"No friend," he answered: "but under this sod
Is the blessed water, the wine of God."

"Water! the Powow is at your back,
And right before you the Merrimac,

"And look you up, or look you down,
There's a well-sweep at every door in town."

"True," he said, "we have wells of our own;
But this I dig for the Lord alone."

Said the other: "This soil is dry, you know.
I doubt if a spring can be found below;

"You had better consult, before you dig,
Some water-witch, with a hazel twig."

"No, wet or dry, I will dig it here,
Shallow or deep, if it takes a year.

"In the Arab desert, where shade is none,
The waterless land of sand and sun,

"Under the pitiless, brazen sky
My burning throat as the sand was dry;

"My crazed brain listened in fever dreams
For plash of buckets and ripple of streams;

"And opening my eyes to the blinding glare,
And my lips to the breath of the blistering air,

"Tortured alike by the heavens and earth,
I cursed, like Job, the day of my birth.

"Then something tender, and sad, and mild
As a mother's voice to her wandering child,

"Rebuked my frenzy; and bowing my head,
I prayed as I never before had prayed:

THE CAPTAIN'S WELL

"Pity me, God! for I die of thirst;
Take me out of this land accurst;

"And if ever I reach my home again,
Where earth has springs, and the sky has rain.

"I will dig a well for the passers-by,
And none shall suffer from thirst as I.

"I saw, as I prayed, my home once more,
The house, the barn, the elms by the door,

"The grass-lined road, that riverward wound,
The tall slate stones of the burying-ground,

"The belfry and steeple on meeting-house hill,
The brook with its dam, and gray grist mill,

"And I knew in that vision beyond the sea,
The very place where my well must be.

"God heard my prayer in that evil day;
He led my feet in their homeward way,

"From false mirage and dried-up well,
And the hot sand storms of a land of hell,

"Till I saw at last through the coast-hill's gap,
A city held in its stony lap,

"The mosques and the domes of scorched Muscat,
And my heart leaped up with joy thereat;

"For there was a ship at anchor lying,
A Christian flag at its mast-head flying,

"And sweetest of sounds to my homesick ear
Was my native tongue in the sailor's cheer.

"Now the Lord be thanked, I am back again,
Where earth has springs, and the skies have rain,

"And the well I promised by Oman's Sea,
I am digging for Him is Amesbury."

His kindred wept, and his neighbors said:
"The poor old captain is out of his head."

But from morn to noon, and from noon to night,
He toiled at his task with main and might;

And when at last, from the loosened earth,
Under his spade the stream gushed forth,

And fast as he climbed to his deep well's brim,
The water he dug for followed him,

He shouted for joy: "I have kept my word,
And here is the well I promised the Lord!"

The long years came and the long years went,
And he sat by his roadside well content;

He watched the travellers, heat-oppressed,
Pause by the way to drink and rest,

And the sweltering horses dip, as they drank,
Their nostrils deep in the cool, sweet tank;

And grateful at heart, his memory went
Back to that waterless Orient,

And the blessed answer of prayer, which came
To the earth of iron and sky of flame.

And when a wayfarer weary and hot,
Kept to the mid-road, pausing not

For the well's refreshing, he shook his head;
"He don't know the value of water," he said;

"Had he prayed for a drop, as I have done,
In the desert circle of sand and sun,

"He would drink and rest, and go home to tell
That God's best gift is the wayside well!"

KATHLEEN

Whittier originally published this ballad as the song of a wandering schoolmaster.

In the 17th century slavery in the New World was not confined to negroes; political offenders and criminals were transported by the British government to Virginia and Barbadoes where they were sold like cattle for work on the plantations. Kidnapping of free and innocent white persons was practiced to a considerable extent in the seaports of the United Kingdom.

O Norah, lay your basket down,
  And rest your weary hand,
And come and hear me sing a song
  Of our old Ireland.

There was a lord of Galaway,
  A mighty lord was he;
And he did wed a second wife,
  A maid of low degree.

KATHLEEN

> But he was old, and she was young,
>   And so, in evil spite,
> She baked the black bread for his kin,
>   And fed her own with white.
>
> She whipped the maids and starved the kern,
>   And drove away the poor;
> "Ah, woe is me!" the old lord said,
>   "I rue my bargain sore!"
>
> This lord he had a daughter fair,
>   Beloved of old and young,
> And nightly round the shealing-fires
>   Of her the gleeman sung.
>
> "As sweet and good is young Kathleen
>   As Eve before her fall;"
> So sang the harper at the fair,
>   So harped he in the hall.
>
> "O come to me, my daughter dear!
>   Come sit upon my knee,
> For looking in your face, Kathleen,
>   Your mother's own I see!"
>
> He smoothed and smoothed her hair away,
>   He kissed her forehead fair;
> "It is my darling Mary's brow,
>   It is my darling's hair!"
>
> O, then spake up the angry dame,
>   "Get up, get up," quoth she,
> "I'll sell ye over Ireland,
>   I'll sell ye o'er the sea!"
>
> She clipped her glossy hair away,
>   That none her rank might know,
> She took away her gown of silk,
>   And gave her one of tow,
>
> And sent her down to Limerick town
>   And to a seaman sold
> This daughter of an Irish lord
>   For ten good pounds in gold.
>
> The lord he smote upon his breast,
>   And tore his beard so gray;
> But he was old, and she was young,
>   And so she had her way.

Sure that same night the Banshee howled
    To fright the evil dame,
And fairy folks, who loved Kathleen,
    With funeral torches came.

She watched them glancing through the trees,
    And glimmering down the hill;
They crept before the dead-vault door,
    And there they all stood still!

"Get up, old man! the wake-lights shine!"
    "Ye murthering witch," quoth he,
"So I'm rid of your tongue, I little care
    If they shine for you or me."

"O, whoso brings my daughter back,
    My gold and land shall have!"
O, then spake up his handsome page,
    "No gold nor land I crave!

"But give to me your daughter dear,
    Give sweet Kathleen to me,
Be she on sea or be she on land,
    I'll bring her back to thee."

"My daughter is a lady born,
    And you of low degree,
But she shall be your bride the day
    You bring her back to me."

He sailed east, he sailed west,
    And far and long sailed he,
Until he came to Boston town,
    Across the great salt sea.

"O, have ye seen the young Kathleen,
    The flower of Ireland?
Ye'll know her by her eyes so blue,
    And by her snow-white hand!"

Out spake an ancient man, "I know
    The maiden whom ye mean;
I bought her of a Limerick man,
    And she is called Kathleen.

"No skill hath she in household work,
    Her hands are soft and white,
Yet well by loving looks and ways
    She doth her cost requite."

So up they walked through Boston town,
    And met a maiden fair,
A little basket on her arm
    So snowy-white and bare.

"Come hither, child, and say hast thou
    This young man ever seen?"
They wept within each other's arms,
    The page and young Kathleen.

"O give to me this darling child,
    And take my purse of gold."
"Nay, not by me," her master said,
    "Shall sweet Kathleen be sold.

"We loved her in the place of one
    The Lord hath early ta'en;
But, since her heart's in Ireland,
    We give her back again!"

O, for that same the saints in heaven
    For his poor soul shall pray,
And Mary Mother wash with tears
    His heresies away.

Sure now they dwell in Ireland,
    As you go up Claremore
Ye'll see their castle looking down
    The pleasant Galway shore.

And the old lord's wife is dead and gone,
    And a happy man is he,
For he sits beside his own Kathleen,
    With her darling on his knee.

CASSANDRA SOUTHWICK

In 1658, Lawrence Southwick, of Salem, Mass., was imprisoned and all of his property forfeited to the government because he had entertained Quakers in his home; his son and daughter were fined for failure to attend church services. When they were unable to pay their fines, the Massachusetts General Court ordered "the Treasurer of the County to sell the said persons to any of the English nations of Virginia or Barbadoes, to answer said fines." An attempt was made to carry this order into execution, but no shipmaster could be found that would take the children to the West Indies to be sold into slavery.

To the God of all sure mercies let my blessing rise today,
From the scoffer and the cruel He hath plucked the spoil
    away,—
Yea, He who cooled the furnace around the faithful three,
And tamed the Chaldean lions, hath set his handmaid free!

Last night I saw the sunset melt through my prison bars,
Last night across my damp earth-floor fell the pale gleam of
    stars;
In the coldness and the darkness all through the long night-
    time,
My grated casement whitened with autumn's early rime.

Alone, in that dark sorrow, hour after hour crept by;
Star after star looked palely in and sank adown the sky;
No sound amid night's stillness, save that which seemed to be
The dull and heavy beating of the pulses of the sea;

All night I sat unsleeping, for I knew that on the morrow
The ruler and the cruel priest would mock me in my sorrow,
Dragged to their place of market, and bargained for and sold,
Like a lamb before the shambles, like a heifer from the fold!

O, the weakness of the flesh was there,—the shrinking and
    the shame;
And the low voice of the Tempter like whispers to me came:
"Why sit'st thou forlornly!" the wicked murmur said,
"Damp walls thy bower of beauty, cold earth thy maiden bed?

"Where be the smiling faces, and voices soft and sweet,
Seen in thy father's dwelling, heard in the pleasant street?
Where be the youths whose glances, the summer Sabbath
    through,
Turned tenderly and timidly unto they father's pew?

"Why sit'st thou here, Cassandra?—Bethink thee with what
    mirth
Thy happy schoolmates gather around the warm bright hearth;
How the crimson shadows tremble on foreheads white and fair,
On eyes of merry girlhood, half hid in golden hair.

"Not for thee the hearth-fire brightens, not for thee kind
    words are spoken,
Not for thee the nuts of Wenham woods by laughing boys
    are broken,
No first-fruits of the orchard within thy lap are laid,
For thee no flowers of autumn the youthful hunters braid.

"O, weak, deluded maiden!—by crazy fancies led,
With wild and raving railers an evil path to tread;

To leave a wholesome worship, and teaching pure and sound;
And mate with maniac women, loose-haired and sackcloth bound.

"Mad scoffers of the priesthood, who mock at things divine,
Who rail against the pulpit, and holy bread and wine;
Sore from their cart-tail scourgings, and from the pillory lame,
Rejoicing in their wretchedness, and glorying in their shame.

"And what a fate awaits thee?—a sadly toiling slave,
Dragging the slowly lengthening chain of bondage to the grave!
Think of thy woman's nature, subdued in hopeless thrall,
The easy prey of any, the scoff and scorn of all!"

O, ever as the Tempter spoke, and feeble Nature's fears
Wrung drop by drop the scalding flow of unavailing tears,
I wrestled down the evil thoughts, and strove in silent prayer,
To feel, O Helper of the weak! that Thou indeed wert there!

I thought of Paul and Silas, within Philippi's cell,
And how from Peter's sleeping limbs the prison-shackles fell,
Till I seemed to hear the trailing of an angel's robe of white,
And to feel a blessed presence invisible to sight.

Bless the Lord for all his mercies!—for the peace and love I felt,
Like dew of Hermon's holy hill, upon my spirit melt;
When "Get behind me, Satan!" was the language of my heart,
And I felt the Evil Tempter with all his doubts depart.

Slow broke the gray cold morning; again the sunshine fell,
Flecked with the shade of bar and grate within my lonely cell;
The hoar-frost melted on the wall, and upward from the street
Came careless laugh and idle word, and tread of passing feet.

At length the heavy bolts fell back, my door was open cast,
And slowly at the sheriff's side, up the long street I passed;
I heard the murmur round me, and felt, but dared not see,
How, from every door and window, the people gazed on me.

And doubt and fear fell on me, shame burned upon my cheek,
Swam earth and sky around me, my trembling limbs grew weak;
"O Lord! support thy handmaid; and from her soul cast out
The fear of man, which brings a snare,—the weakness and the doubt."

Then the dreary shadows scattered, like a cloud in morning's
  breeze,
And a low deep voice within me seemed whispering words like
  these:
Though thy earth be as the iron, and thy heaven a brazen
  wall,
Trust still His loving-kindness whose power is over all."

We paused at length, where at my feet the sunlit waters broke
On glaring reach of shining beach, and shingly wall of rock;
The merchant-ships lay idly there, in hard clear lines on high,
Tracing with rope and slender spar their network on the sky.

And there were ancient citizens, cloak-wrapped and grave and
  cold,
And grim and stout sea-captains with faces bronzed and old,
And on his horse, with Rawson, his cruel clerk at hand,
Sat dark and haughty Endicott, the ruler of the land.

And poisoning with his evil words the ruler's ready ear,
The priest leaned o'er his saddle, with laugh and scoff and
  jeer;
It stirred my soul, and from my lips the seal of silence broke,
As if through woman's weakness a warning spirit spoke.

I cried, "The Lord rebuke thee, thou smiter of the meek,
Thou robber of the righteous, thou trampler of the weak!
Go light the dark, cold hearth-stones,—go turn the prison lock
Of the poor hearts thou hast hunted, thou wolf amid the
  flock!"

Dark lowered the brows of Endicott, and with a deeper red
O'er Rawson's wine-empurpled cheek the flush of anger spread;
"Good people," quoth the white-lipped priest, "heed not her
  words so wild,
Her Master speaks within her,—the Devil owns his child!"

But gray heads shook, and young brows knit, the while the
  sheriff read
That law the wicked rulers against the poor have made,
Who to their house of Rimmon and idol priesthood bring
No bended knee of worship, nor gainful offering.

Then to the stout sea-captains the sheriff, turning, said,—
"Which of ye, worthy seamen, will take this Quaker maid?
In the Isle of fair Barbadoes, or on Virginia's shore,
You may hold her at a higher price than Indian girl or Moor."

Grim and silent stood the captains; and when again he cried,
"Speak out, my worthy seamen!"—no voice, no sign replied;

CASSANDRA SOUTHWICK

But I felt a hard hand press my own, and kind words met my ear,—
"God bless thee, and preserve thee, my gentle girl and dear!"

A weight seemed lifted from my heart,—a pitying friend was nigh,
I felt it in his hard, rough hand, and saw it in his eye;
And when again the sheriff spoke, that voice, so kind to me,
Growled back its stormy answer like the roaring of the sea,—

"Pile my ship with bars of silver,—pack with coins of Spanish gold,
From keel-piece up to deck-plank, the roomage of her hold,
By the living God who made me!—I would sooner in your bay
Sink ship and crew and cargo, than bear this child away!"

"Well answered, worthy captain, shame on their cruel laws!"
Ran through the crowd in murmurs loud the people's just applause.
"Like the herdsman of Tekoa, in Israel of old,
Shall we see the poor and righteous again for silver sold?"

I looked on haughty Endicott; with weapon half-way drawn,
Swept round the throng his lion glare of bitter hate and scorn;
Fiercely he drew his bridle-rein, and turned in silence back,
And sneering priest and baffled clerk rode murmuring in his track.

Hard after them the sheriff looked, in bitterness of soul;
Thrice smote his staff upon the ground, and crushed his parchment roll.
"Good friends," he said, "since both have fled, the ruler and the priest,
Judge ye, if from their further work I be not well released."

Loud was the cheer which, full and clear, swept round the silent bay,
As, with kind words and kinder looks, he bade me go my way;
For He who turns the courses of the streamlet of the glen,
And the river of great waters, had turned the hearts of men.

O, at that hour the very earth seemed changed beneath my eye,
A holier wonder round me rose the blue walls of the sky,
A lovelier light on rock and hill and stream and woodland lay,
And softer lapsed on sunnier sands the waters of the bay.

Thanksgiving to the Lord of life!—to Him all praises be,
Who from the hands of evil men hath set his handmaid free;

All praise to Him before whose power the mighty are afraid,
Who takes the crafty in the snare which for the poor is laid!

Sing, O my soul, rejoicingly, on evening's twilight calm
Uplift the loud thanksgiving,—pour forth the grateful psalm;
Let all dear hearts with me rejoice, as did the saints of old,
When of the Lord's good angel the rescued Peter told.

And weep and howl, ye evil priests and mighty men of wrong,
The Lord shall smite the proud, and lay his hand upon the strong.
Woe to the wicked rulers in his avenging hour!
Woe to the wolves who seek the flocks to raven and devour!

But let the humble ones arise,—the poor in heart be glad,
And let the mourning ones again with robes of praise be clad,
For He who cooled the furnace, and smoothed the stormy wave,
And tamed the Chaldean lions, is mighty still to save!

HOW THE WOMEN WENT FROM DOVER

In 1662, the following warrant was issued by Major Waldron of Dover, N. H., "To the Constables of Dover, Hampton, Salisbury, Newbury, Rowley, Ipswich, Wenham, Lynn, Boston, Roxbury, Dedham and until these vagabond Quakers are carried out of this jurisdiction.

"You, and every one of you, are required, in the King's Majesty's name, to take these vagabond Quakers, Anne Colman, Mary Tomkins and Alice Ambrose, and make them fast to the cart's tail, and driving the cart through your several towns, to whip them upon their naked backs not exceeding ten stripes apiece on each of them, in each town; and so to convey them from constable to constable till they are out of this jurisdiction, as you will answer it at your peril, and this shall be your warrant."

RICHARD WALDRON

Dated at Dover, December 22, 1662"

The warrant was executed only in Dover and Hampton, N. H. The Salisbury constable refused to obey the warrant and he was supported by the townspeople and Major Robert Pike, then the leader in that part of the County, and who was one of the leaders for religious freedom and far ahead of his time. In 1692, he wrote a letter to the judges at Salem remonstrating against the witch-craft trials.

HOW THE WOMEN WENT FROM DOVER

The tossing spray of Cocheco's fall
Hardened to ice on its rocky wall,
As through Dover town in the chill, gray dawn,
Three women passed, at the cart-tail drawn!

Bared to the waist, for the north wind's grip
And keener sting of the constable's whip,
The blood that followed each hissing blow
Froze as it sprinkled the winter snow.

Priest and ruler, boy and maid
Followed the dismal cavalcade;
And from door and window, open thrown,
Looked and wondered gaffer and crone.

"God is our witness," the victims cried,
"We suffer for Him who for all men died;
The wrong ye do has been done before,
We bear the stripes that the Master bore!

And thou, O Richard Waldron, for whom
We hear the feet of a coming doom,
On thy cruel heart and thy hand of wrong
Vengeance is sure, though it tarry long.

"In the light of the Lord, a flame we see
Climb and kindle a proud roof-tree;
And beneath it an old man lying dead,
With stains of blood on his hoary head."

"Smite, Goodman Hate-Evil!—harder still!"
The magistrate cried, "lay on with a will!
Drive out of their bodies the Father of Lies,
Who through them preaches and prophesies!"

So into the forest they held their way,
By winding river and frost-rimmed bay,
Over wind-swept hills that felt the beat
Of the winter sea at their icy feet.

The Indian hunter, searching his traps,
Peered stealthily through the forest gaps;
And the outlying settler shook his head,—
"They're witches going to jail," he said.

At last a meeting-house came in view;
A blast on his horn the constable blew;
And the boys of Hampton cried up and down,
"The Quakers have come!" to the wondering town.

From barn and woodpile the goodman came;
The goodwife quitted her quilting frame,
With her child at her breast; and, hobbling slow,
The grandam followed to see the show.

Once more the torturing whip was swung,
Once more keen lashes the bare flesh stung.
"Oh, spare! they are bleeding!" a little maid cried,
And covered her face the sight to hide.

A murmur ran round the crowd: "Good folks,"
Quoth the constable, busy counting the strokes,
"No pity to wretches like these is due,
They have beaten the gospel black and blue!"

Then a pallid woman, in wild-eyed fear,
With her wooden noggin of milk drew near.
"Drink, poor hearts!" a rude hand smote
Her draught away from a parching throat.

"Take heed," one whispered, "they'll take your cow
For fines, as they took your horse and plow,
And the bed from under you." "Even so,"
She said. "They are cruel as death, I know."

Then on they passed, in the waning day,
Through Seabrook woods, a weariful way;
By great salt meadows and sand-hills bare,
And glimpses of blue sea here and there.

By the meeting-house in Salisbury town,
The sufferers stood, in the red sundown,
Bare for the lash! O pitying Night,
Drop swift thy curtain and hide the sight!

With shame in his eye and wrath on his lip
The Salisbury constable dropped his whip.
"This warrant means murder foul and red;
Cursed is he who serves it," he said.

"Show me the order, and meanwhile strike
A blow at your peril!" said Justice Pike.
Of all rulers the land possessed,
Wisest and boldest was he and best.

He scoffed at witchcraft; the priest he met
As man meets man; his feet he set
Beyond his dark age, standing upright,
Soul-free, with his face to the morning light.

He read the warrant: "These convey
From our precincts; at every town on the way
Give each ten lashes." "God judge the brute!
I tread his order under my foot!

"Cut loose these poor ones and let them go;
Come what will of it, all men shall know
No warrant is good, though backed by the Crown,
For whipping women in Salisbury town!"

The hearts of the villagers, half released
From creed of terror and rule of priest,
By a primal instinct owned the right
Of human pity in law's despite.

For ruth and chivalry only slept,
His Saxon manhood the yeoman kept;
Quicker or slower, the same blood ran
In the Cavalier and the Puritan.

The Quakers sank on their knees in praise
And thanks. A last, low sunset blaze
Flashed out from under a cloud, and shed
A golden glory on each bowed head.

The tale is one of an evil time,
When souls were fettered and thought was crime,
And heresy's whisper above its breath
Meant shameful scourging and bonds and death!

What marvel, that hunted and sorely tried,
Even woman rebuked and prophesied,
And soft words rarely answered back
The grim persuasion of whip and rack!

If her cry from the whipping-post and jail
Pierced sharp as the Kenite's driven nail,
O woman, at ease in these happier days,
Forbear to judge of thy sister's ways!

How much thy beautiful life may owe
To her faith and courage thou canst not know,
Nor how from the paths of thy calm retreat
She smoothed the thorns with her bleeding feet.

MARGUERITE
Massachusetts Bay in 1760

The robins sang in the orchard, the buds into blossoms grew;
Little of human sorrow the buds and the robins knew!

Sick, in an alien household, the poor French neutral lay;
Into her lonesome garret fell the light of the April day.

Through the dusty window, curtained by the spider's warp and woof,
On the loose-laid floor of hemlock, on oaken ribs of roof.

The bedquilt's faded patchwork, the teacups on the stand,
The wheel with flaxen tangle, as it dropped from her sick hand!

What to her was the song of the robin, or warm morning light,
As she lay in the trance of the dying, heedless of sound or sight?

Done was the work of her hands, she had eaten her bitter bread;
The world of the alien people lay behind her dim and dead.

But her soul went back to its child-time; she saw the sun o'erflow
With gold the basin of Minas, and set over Gasperau;

The low, bare flats at ebb-tide, the rush of the sea at flood,
Through inlet and creek and river, from dike to upland wood;

The gulls in the red of morning, the fish-hawk's rise and fall,
The drift of the fog in moonshine, over the dark coast-wall.

She saw the face of her mother, she heard the song she sang;
And far off, faintly, slowly, the bell for vespers rang!

By her bed the hard-faced mistress sat, smoothing the wrinkled sheet,
Peering into the face, so helpless, and feeling the ice-cold feet.

With a vague remorse atoning for her greed and long abuse,
By care no longer heeded and pity too late for use.

Up the stairs of the garret softly the son of the mistress stepped,
Leaned over the head-board, covering his face with his hands, and wept.

Outspake the mother, who watched him sharply, with brow a-frown:
"What! love you the Papist, the beggar, the charge of the town?"

"Be she Papist or beggar who lies here, I know and God knows
I love her, and fain would go with her wherever she goes!

"O mother! that sweet face came pleading, for love so athirst.
You saw but the town-charge; I knew her God's angel at
   first."

Shaking her gray head, the mistress hushed down a bitter cry;
And awed by the silence and shadow of death drawing nigh,

She murmured a psalm of the Bible; but closer the young girl
   pressed,
With the last of her life in her fingers, the cross to her breast.

"My son, come away," cried the mother, her voice cruel grown.
"She is joined to her idols, like Ephraim; let her alone!"

But he knelt with his hand on her forehead, his lips to her
   ear,
And he called back the soul that was passing: "Marguerite, do
   you hear?"

She paused on the threshold of Heaven; love, pity, surprise,
Wistful, tender lit up for an instant the cloud of her eyes.

With his heart on his lips he kissed her, but never her cheek
   grew red,
And the words the living long for he spake in the ear of the
   dead.

And the robins sang in the orchard, where buds to blossoms
   grew;
Of the folded hands and the still face never the robins knew!

THE WITCH OF WENHAM
I
Along Crane River's sunny slopes,
   Blew warm the winds of May,
And over Naumkeag's ancient oaks
   The green outgrew the gray.

The grass was green on Rial-side,
   The early birds at will
Waked up the violet in its dell,
   The wind-flower on its hill.

"Where go you, in your Sunday coat
   Son Andrew, tell me, pray."
"For striped perch in Wenham Lake
   I go to fish to-day."

"Unharmed of thee in Wenham Lake
   The mottled perch shall be:
A blue-eyed witch sits on the bank
   And weaves her net for thee.

"She weaves her golden hair; she sings
    Her spell-song low and faint;
The wickedest witch in Salem jail
    Is to that girl a saint."

"Nay, mother, hold thy cruel tongue;
    God knows," the young man cried,
"He never made a whiter soul
    Than hers by Wenham side.

"She tends her mother sick and blind,
    And every want supplies;
To her above the blessed Book
    She lends her soft blue eyes.

"Her voice is glad with holy songs,
    Her lips are sweet with prayer;
Go where you will, in ten miles round
    Is none more good and fair."

"Son Andrew, for the love of God
    And of thy mother, stay!"
She clapsed her hands, she wept aloud,
    But Andrew rode away.

"O reverend sir, my Andrew's soul
    The Wenham witch has caught;
She holds him with his curled gold
    Whereof her snare is wrought.

"She charms him with her great blue eyes,
    She binds him with her hair;
Oh, break the spell with holy words,
    Unbind him with a prayer!"

"Take heart," the painful preacher said,
    "This mischief shall not be;
The witch shall perish in her sins
    And Andrew shall go free.

"Our poor Ann Putnam testifies
    She saw her weave a spell,
Bare-armed, loose-haired, at full of moon,
    Around a dried-up well.

" 'Spring up, O well!' she softly sang
    The Hebrew's old refrain
(For Satan uses Bible words),
    Till water flowed amain.

"And many a goodwife heard her speak
    By Wenham water words
That made the buttercups take wings
    And turn to yellow birds.

"They say that swarming wild bees seek
    The hive at her command:
And fishes swim to take their food
    From out her dainty hand.

"Meek as she sits in meeting-time,
    The godly minister
Notes well the spell that doth compel
    The young men's eyes to her.

"The mole upon her dimpled chin
    Is Satan's seal and sign;
Her lips are red with evil bread
    And stain of unblest wine.

"For Tituba, my Indian, saith
    At Quasycung she took
The Black Man's godless sacrament
    And signed his dreadful book.

"Last night my sore-afflicted child
    Against the young witch cried.
To take her Marshal Herrick rides
    Even now to Wenham side."

The marshal in his saddle sat,
    His daughter at his knee;
"I go to fetch that arrant witch,
    Thy fair playmate," quoth he.

"Her spectre walks the parsonage,
    And haunts both hall and stair;
They know her by the great blue eyes
    And floating gold of hair."

"They lie, they lie, my father dear!
    No foul old witch is she,
But sweet and good and crystal-pure
    As Wenham waters be."

"I tell thee, child, the Lord hath set
    Before us good and ill,
And woe to all whose carnal loves
    Oppose His righteous will.

"Between Him and the powers of hell
    Choose thou, my child, to-day:
No sparing hand, no pitying eye,
    When God commands to slay!"

He went his way; the old wives shook
    With fear as he drew nigh;
The children in the dooryards held
    Their breath as he passed by.

Too well they knew the gaunt gray horse
    The grim witch-hunter rode—
The pale Apocalyptic beast
    By grisly Death bestrode.

II.

Oh, fair the face of Wenham Lake
    Upon the young girl's shone,
Her tender mouth, her dreaming eye,
    Her yellow hair outblown.

By happy youth and love attuned
    To natural harmonies,
The singing birds, the whispering wind,
    She sat beneath the trees.

Sat shaping for her bridal dress
    Her mother's wedding gown,
When lo! the marshal, writ in hand,
    From Alford hill rode down.

His face was hard with cruel fear,
    He grasped the maiden's hands;
"Come with me unto Salem town,
    For so the law commands!"

"Oh, let me to my mother say
    Farewell before I go!"
He closer tied her little hands
    Unto his saddle bow.

"Unhand me," cried she piteously,
    "For thy sweet daughter's sake."
"I'll keep my daughter safe," he said,
    "From the witch of Wenham Lake."

"Oh, leave me for my mother's sake,
    She needs my eyes to see."
"Those eyes, young witch, the crows shall peck
    From off the gallows-tree."

He bore her to a farm-house old,
  And up its stairway long,
And closed on her the garret-door
  With iron bolted strong.

The day died out, the night came down;
  Her evening prayer she said,
While, through the dark, strange faces seemed
  To mock her as she prayed.

The present horror deepened all
  The fears her childhood knew:
The awe wherewith the air was filled
  With every breath she drew.

And could it be, she trembling asked,
  Some secret thought or sin
Had shut good angels from her heart
  And let the bad ones in?

Had she in some forgotten dream
  Let go her hold on Heaven,
And sold herself unwittingly
  To spirits unforgiven?

Oh, weird and still the dark hours passed;
  No human sound she heard,
But up and down the chimney stack
  The swallows moaned and stirred.

And o'er her, with a dread surmise
  Of evil sight and sound,
The blind bats on their leathern wings
  Went wheeling round and round.

Low hanging in the midnight sky
  Looked in a half-faced moon.
Was it a dream, or did she hear
  Her lover's whistled tune?

She forced the oaken scuttle back;
  A whisper reached her ear:
"Slide down the roof to me," it said,
  "So softly none may hear."

She slid along the sloping roof
  Till from its eaves she hung,
And felt the loosened shingles yield
  To which her fingers clung.

Below, her lover stretched his hands
    And touched her feet so small;
"Drop down to me, dear heart," he said,
    "My arms shall break the fall."

He set her on his pillion soft,
    Her arms about him twined;
And, noiseless as if velvet-shod,
    They left the house behind.

But when they reached the open way
    Full free the rein he cast;
Oh, never through the mirk midnight
    Rode man and maid more fast.

Along the wild wood-paths they sped,
    The bridgeless streams they swam;
At set of moon they passed the Bass,
    At sunrise Agawam.

At high noon on the Merrimac
    The ancient ferryman
Forgot, at times, his idle oars,
    So fair a freight to scan.

And when from off his grounded boat
    He saw them mount and ride,
"God keep her from the evil eye,
    And harm of witch!" he cried.

The maiden laughed, as youth will laugh
    At all its fears gone by;
"He does not know," she whispered low,
    "A little witch am I."

All day he urged his weary horse,
    And, in the red sundown,
Drew rein before a friendly door
    In distant Berwick town.

A fellow-feeling for the wronged
    The Quaker people felt;
And safe beside their kindly hearths
    The hunted maiden dwelt,

Until from off its breast the land
    The haunting horrow threw,
And hatred, born of ghastly dreams,
    To shame and pity grew.

Sad were the year's spring morns, and sad
  Its golden summer day,
But blithe and glad its withered fields,
  And skies of ashen gray;

For spell and charm had power no more,
  The spectre ceased to roam,
And scattered households knelt again
  Around the hearths of home.

And when once more by Beaver Dam
  The meadow-lark outsang,
And once again on all the hills
  The early violets sprang,

And all the windy pasture slopes
  Lay green within the arms
Of creeks that bore the salted sea
  To pleasant inland farms,

The smith filed off the chains he forged,
  The jail-bolts backward fell;
And youth and hoary age came forth
  Like souls escaped from hell.

THE KING'S MISSIVE

Governor Endicott was forced by Royal decree in 1661, to release persecuted Quakers then imprisoned. The decree was brought to this country by Shattuck, a Quaker, who delivered the decree to the Governor at his residence and not, as stated in the poem, in the Council Chamber.

Under the great hill sloping bare
  To cove and meadow and Common lot,
In his council chamber and oaken chair,
  Sat the worshipful Governor Endicott.
A grave, strong man, who knew no peer
In the pilgrim land, where he ruled in fear
Of God, not man, and for good or ill
Held his trust with an iron will.

He had shorn with his sword the cross from out
  The flag, and cloven the May-pole down,
Harried the heathen round about,
  And whipped the Quakers from town to town.
Earnest and honest, a man at need
To burn like a torch for his own harsh creed,
He kept with the flaming brand of his zeal
The gate of the holy common weal.

His brow was clouded, his eye was stern,
    With a look of mingled sorrow and wrath;
"Woe's me!" he murmured: "At every turn
    The pestilent Quakers are in my path!
Some we have scourged, and banished some,
Some hanged, more doomed, and still they come,
Fast as the tide of yon bay sets in,
Sowing their heresy's need of sin.

"Did we count on this? Did we leave behind
    The graves of our kin, the comfort and ease
Of our English hearths and homes, to find
    Troublers of Israel such as these?
Shall I spare? Shall I pity them? God forbid!
I will do as the prophet to Agag did:
They come to poison the wells of the Word,
I will hew them in pieces before the Lord!"

The door swung open, and Rawson the clerk
    Entered, and whispered under breath.
"There waits below for the hangman's work
    A fellow banished on pain of death—
Shattuck, of Salem, unhealed of the whip,
Brought over in Master Goldsmith's ship
At anchor here in a Christian port,
With freight of the devil and all his sort!"

Twice and thrice on the chamber floor
    Striding fiercely from wall to wall,
"The Lord do so to me and more,"
    The Governor cried, "if I hang not all!
Bring hither the Quaker." Calm, sedate,
With the look of a man at ease with fate,
Into that presence grim and dread
Came Samuel Shattuck, with hat on head.

"Off with the knave's hat!" An angry hand
    Smote down the offence; but the wearer said,
With a quiet smile, "By the king's command
    I bear his message and stand in his stead."
In the Governor's hand a missive he laid
With the royal arms on its seal displayed,
And the proud man spake as he gazed thereat,
Uncovering, "Give Mr. Shattuck his hat."

He turned to the Quaker, bowing low,—
    "The king commandeth your friends' release,
Doubt not he shall be obeyed, although
    To his subjects' sorrow and sin's increase.

THE KING'S MISSIVE

What he here enjoineth, John Endicott,
His loyal servant, questioneth not.
You are free! God grant the spirit you own
May take you from us to parts unknown."

So the door of the jail was open cast,
    And, like Daniel, out of the lion's den
Tender youth and girlhood passed,
    With age-bowed women and gray-locked men.
And the voice of one appointed to die
Was lifted in praise and thanks on high.
And the little maid from New Netherlands
Kissed, in her joy, the doomed man's hands.

And one, whose call was to minister
    To the souls in prison, beside him went,
An ancient woman, bearing with her
    The linen shroud for his burial meant.
For she, not counting her own life dear,
In the strength of a love that cast out fear,
Had watched and served where her brethren died,
Like those who waited the cross beside.

One moment they paused on their way to look
    On the martyr graves by the Common-side.
And much scourged Wharton of Salem took
    His burden of prophecy up and cried:
"Rest, souls of the valiant! Not in vain
Have ye borne the Master's cross of pain;
Ye have fought the fight, ye are victors crowned,
With a fourfold chain ye have Satan bound!"

The autumn haze lay soft and still
    On wood and meadow and upland farms;
On the brow of Snow Hill the great windmill
    Slowly and lazily swung its arms;
Broad in the sunshine stretched away
With its capes and islands, the turquoise bay;
And over water and dusk of pines
Blue hills lifted their faint outlines.

The topaz leaves of the walnut glowed,
    The sumach added its crimson fleck,
And double in air and water showed
    The tinted maples along the Neck;
Through frost flower clusters of pale star-mist,
And gentian fringes of amethyst,
And royal plumes of golden-rod,
The grazing cattle on Centry trod.

But as they who see not, the Quakers saw
    The world about them; they only thought
With deep thanksgiving and pious awe
    On the great deliverance God had wrought.
Through lane and alley the gazing town
Noisily followed them up and down;
Some with scoffing and brutal jeer,
Some with pity and words of cheer.

One brave voice rose above the din.
    Upsall, gray with his length of days,
Cried from the door of his Red Lion Inn:
    "Men of Boston, give God the praise!
No more shall innocent blood call down
The bolts of wrath on your guilty town.
The freedom of worship, dear to you,
Is dear to all, and to all is due.

"I see the vision of days to come,
    When your beautiful City of the Bay
Shall be Christian liberty's chosen home,
    And none shall his neighbor's rights gainsay.
The varying notes of worship shall blend
And as one great prayer to God ascend,
And hands of mutual charity raise
Walls of salvation and gates of praise."

So passed the Quakers through Boston town,
    Whose painful ministers sighed to see
The walls of their sheep-fold falling down,
    And wolves of heresy prowling free.
But the years went on, and brought no wrong;
With milder counsels the State grew strong.
As outward Letter and inward Light
Kept the balance of truth aright.

The Puritan spirit perishing not,
    To Concord's yeomen the signal sent,
And spake in the voice of the cannon-shot
    That severed the chains of a continent.
With its gentler mission of peace and good-will
The thought of the Quaker is living still,
And the freedom of soul he prophesied
Is gospel and law where the martyrs died.

THE WRECK AT RIVERMOUTH

Goody Cole, the Hampton witch mentioned in this poem, died a natural death, but the citizens of Hampton, N. H.,

THE WRECK AT RIVERMOUTH

buried her with a stake through her body to keep her down in her grave.

    Rivermouth Rocks are fair to see,
        By dawn or sunset shone across,
    When the ebb of the sea has left them free,
        To dry their fringes of gold-green moss:
    For there the river comes winding down
    From salt sea-meadows and uplands brown,
    And waves on the outer rocks afoam
    Shout to its waters, "Welcome home!"

    And fair are the sunny isles in view
        East of the grisly Head of the Boar,
    And Agamenticus lifts its blue
        Disk of a cloud the woodlands o'er;
    And southerly, when the tide is down,
    "Twixt white sea-waves and sand-hills brown,
    The beach-birds dance and the gray gulls wheel
    Over a floor of burnished steel.

    Once, in the old Colonial days,
        Two hundred years ago and more,
    A boat sailed down through the winding ways
        Of Hampton River to that low shore,
    Full of a goodly company
    Sailing out on the summer sea,
    Veering to catch the land-breeze light,
    With the Boar to left and the Rocks to right.

    In Hampton meadows, where mowers laid
        Their scythes to the swaths of salted grass,
    "Ah, well-a-day! our hay must be made!"
        A young man sighed, who saw them pass.
    Loud laughed his fellows to see him stand
    Whetting his scythe with a listless hand,
    Hearing a voice in a far-off song,
    Watching a white hand beckoning long.

    "Fie on the witch!" cried a merry girl,
        As they rounded the point where Goody Cole
    Sat by her door with her wheel atwirl,
        A bent and blear-eyed poor old soul.
    "Oho!" she muttered, "ye're brave to-day
    But I hear the little waves laugh and say,
    'The broth will be cold that waits at home;
    For it's one to go, but another to come!'"

THE WRECK AT RIVERMOUTH

"She's cursed," said the skipper; "speak her fair:
    I'm scary always to see her shake
Her wicked head, with its wild gray hair,
    And nose like a hawk, and eyes like a snake."
But merrily still, with a laugh and shout,
From Hampton River the boat sailed out,
Till the huts and the flakes on Star seemed nigh,
And they lost the scent of the pines of Rye.

They dropped their lines in the lazy tide,
    Drawing up haddock and mottled cod,
They saw not the Shadow that walked beside,
    They heard not the feet with silence shod.
But thicker and thicker a hot mist grew,
Shot by the lightnings through and through;
And muffled growls, like the growl of a beast,
Ran along the sky from west to east.

Then the skipper looked from the darkening sea
    Up to the dimmed and wading sun;
But he spake like a brave man cheerily,
    "Yet there is time for our homeward run."
Veering and tacking, they backward wore;
And just as a breath from the woods ashore
Blew out to whisper of danger past,
The wrath of the storm came down at last!

The skipper hauled at the heavy sail:
    "God be our help!" he only cried,
As the roaring gale, like the stroke of a flail,
    Smote the boat on its starboard side.
The Shoalsmen looked, but saw alone
Dark films of rain-cloud slantwise blown,
Wild rocks lit up by the lightning's glare,
The strife and torment of sea and air.

Goody Cole looked out from her door:
    The Isles of Shoals were drowned and gone,
Scarcely she saw the Head of the Boar
    Toss the foam from tusks of stone.
She clasped her hands with a grip of pain,
The tear on her cheek was not of rain:
"They are lost," she muttered, "boat and crew!
Lord, forgive me! my words were true!"

Suddenly seaward swept the squall;
    The low sun smote through cloudy rack;
The Shoals stood clear in the light, and all
    The trend of the coast lay hard and black.

THE WRECK AT RIVERMOUTH

But far and wide as eye could reach,
No life was seen upon wave or beach;
The boat that went out at morning never
Sailed back again into Hampton River.

O mower, lean on thy bended snath,
  Look from the meadows green and low:
The wind of the sea is a waft of death,
  The waves are singing a song of woe!
By silent river, by moaning sea,
Long and vain shall thy watching be:
Never again shall the sweet voice call,
Never the white hand rise and fall!

O Rivermouth Rocks, how sad a sight
  Ye saw in the light of breaking day!
Dead faces looking up cold and white
  From sand and sea-weed where they lay.
The mad old witch-wife wailed and wept,
And cursed the tide as it backward crept;
"Crawl back, crawl back, blue water-snake!
Leave your dead for the hearts that break!"

Solemn it was in that old day
  In Hampton town and its log-built church,
Where side by side the coffins lay
  And the mourners stood in aisle and porch.
In the singing-seats young eyes were dim,
The voices faltered that raised the hymn,
And Father Dalton, grave and stern,
Sobbed through his prayer and wept in turn.

But his ancient colleague did not pray,
  Because of his sin at fourscore years:
He stood apart, with the iron-gray
  Of his strong brows knitted to hide his tears.
And a wretched woman, holding her breath
In the awful presence of sin and death,
Cowered and shrank, while her neighbors thronged
To look on the dead her shame had wronged.

Apart with them, like them forbid,
  Old Goody Cole looked drearily round,
As, two by two, with their faces hid,
  The mourners walked to the burying-ground.
She let the staff from her clasped hands fall:
"Lord, forgive us! we're sinners all!"
And the voice of the old man answered her:
"Amen!" said Father Bachiler.

So, as I sat upon Appledore
    In the calm of a closing summer day,
And the broken lines of Hampton shore
    In purple mist of cloudland lay,
The Rivermouth Rocks their story told;
And waves aglow with sunset gold,
Rising and breaking in steady chime,
Beat the rhythm and kept the time.

And the sunset paled, and warmed once more
    With a softer, tenderer after-glow;
In the east was moon-rise, with boats off-shore
    And sails in the distance drifting slow.
The beacon glimmered from Portsmouth bar,
The White Isle kindled its great red star;
And life and death in my old-time lay
Mingled in peace like the night and day!

"Well!" said the Man of Books, "your story
    Is really not ill told in verse.
As the Celt said of purgatory,
    'One might go farther and fare worse.'
    The Reader smiled; and once again
    With steadier voice took up his strain,
While the fair singer from the neighboring tent
Drew near, and at his side a graceful listener bent.

THE NEW WIFE AND THE OLD

General Moulton of Hampton, N. H., married a young and beautiful girl for his second wife; and on their wedding night the abused first wife returned to snatch the rings from the second wife's fingers. Moulton had sold his soul to the Devil for a bootful of gold that was to be poured down the chimney until the boot was full; Moulton cut off the toe of his boot and the Devil was unable to fill it as the gold ran into the room. The Devil was so angry at being tricked that he cursed the farm and when Moulton died he turned the corpse into a big black rock so heavy that the pall bearers were unable to lift the coffin. Moulton was reputed to have been a local racketeer who wrecked ships by hanging false lights on the Hampton rivermouth rocks to lure storm-driven vessels ashore, in the belief they were making either Portsmouth or Newburyport harbor.

    Dark the halls, and cold the feast,—
    Gone the bridesmaids, gone the priest:

THE NEW WIFE AND THE OLD

All is over,—all is done,
Twain of yesterday are one!
Blooming girl and manhood gray,
Autumn in the arms of May!

Hushed within and hushed without,
Dancing feet and wrestlers' shout;
Dies the bonfire on the hill;
All is dark and all is still,
Save the starlight, save the breeze
Moaning through the graveyard trees;
And the great sea-waves below,
Pulse of the midnight beating slow.

From the brief dream of a bride
She hath wakened, at his side.
With half-uttered shriek and start,—
Feels she not his beating heart?
And the pressure of his arm,
And his breathing near and warm?

Lightly from the bridal bed
Springs that fair dishevelled head,
And a feeling, new, intense,
Half of shame, half innocence,
Maiden fear and wonder speaks
Through her lips and changing cheeks.

From the oaken mantel glowing
Faintest light the lamp is throwing
On the mirror's antique mould,
High-backed chair, and wainscot old,
And, through faded curtains stealing,
His dark sleeping face revealing.

Listless lies the strong man there,
Silver-streaked his careless hair;
Lips of love have left no trace
On that hard and haughty face;
And that forehead's knitted thought
Love's soft hand hath not unwrought.

"Yet," she sighs, "he loves me well,
More than these calm lips will tell.
Stooping to my lowly state,
He hath made me rich and great,
And I bless him, though he be
Hard and stern to all save me!"

While she speaketh, falls the light
O'er her fingers small and white;
Gold and gem, and costly ring
Back the timid lustre fling,—
Love's selectest gifts, and rare,
His proud hand had fastened there.

Gratefully she marks the glow
From those tapering lines of snow;
Fondly o'er the sleeper bending
His black hair with golden blending,
In her soft and light caress,
Cheek and lip together press.

Ha!—that start of horror!—Why
That wild stare and wilder cry,
Full of terror, full of pain?
Is there madness in her brain?
Hark! that gasping, hoarse and low,
"Spare me,—spare me,—let me go "

God have mercy,—Icy cold
Spectral hands her own enfold,
Drawing silently from them
Love's fair gifts of gold and gem,
"Waken! save me!" still as death
At her side he slumbereth.

Ring and bracelet all are gone,
And that ice-cold hand withdrawn;
But she hears a murmur low,
Full of sweetness, full of woe,
Half a sigh and half a moan:
"Fear not! give the dead her own!"

Ah!—the dead wife's voice she knows!
That cold hand, whose pressure froze,
Once in warmest life had borne
Gem and band her own hath worn.
"Wake thee! wake thee!" Lo, his eyes
Open with a dull surprise.

In his arms the strong man folds her,
Closer to his breast he holds her;
Trembling limbs his own are meeting,
And he feels her heart's quick beating:
"Nay my dearest, why this fear?"
"Hush!" she saith, "the dead is here!"

THE NEW WIFE AND THE OLD

"Nay, a dream,—an idle dream."
But before the lamp's pale gleam
Tremblingly her hand she raises,—
There no more the diamond blazes,
Clasp of pearl, or ring of gold,—
"Ah!" she sighs, "her hand was cold!"

Broken words of cheer he saith,
But his dark lip quivereth,
And as o'er the past he thinketh,
From his young wife's arms he shrinketh;
Can those soft arms round him lie,
Underneath his dead wife's eye?

She her fair young head can rest
Soothed and childlike on his breast,
And in trustful innocence
Draw new strength and courage thence;
He, the proud man, feels within
But the cowardice of sin!

She can murmur in her thought
Simple prayers her mother taught,
And His blessed angels call,
Whose great love is over all;
He, alone, in prayerless pride,
Meets the dark Past at her side!

One, who living shrank with dread
From his look, or word, or tread,
Unto whom her early grave
Was as freedom to the slave,
Moves him at this midnight hour,
With the dead's unconscious power!

Ah, the dead, the unforgot!
From their solemn homes of thought,
Where the cypress shadows blend
Darkly over foe and friend,
Or in love or sad rebuke,
Back upon the living look.

And the tenderest ones and weakest,
Who their wrongs have borne the meekest,
Lifting from those dark, still places,
Sweet and sad-remembered faces,
O'er the guilty hearts behind
An unwitting triumph find.

THE THREE BELLS

Beneath the low-hung night cloud
    That raked her splintering mast
The good ship settled slowly,
    The cruel leak gained fast.

Over the awful ocean
    Her signal guns pealed out.
Dear God! was that thy answer
    From the horror round about?

A voice came down the wild wind,
    "Ho! ship ahoy!" its cry:
"Our stout Three Bells of Glasgow
    Shall lay till daylight by!"

Hour after hour crept slowly,
    Yet on the heaving swells
Tossed up and down the ship-lights,
    The lights of the Three Bells!

And ship to ship made signals,
    Man answered back to man,
While oft, to cheer and hearten,
    The Three Bells nearer ran;

And the captain from her taffrail
    Sent down his hopeful cry.
"Take heart! Hold on!" he shouted.
    "The Three Bells shall lay by!"

All night across the waters
    The tossing lights shone clear;
All night from reeling taffrail
    The Three Bells sent her cheer.

And when the dreary watches
    Of storm and darkness passed,
Just as the wreck lurched under
    All souls were saved at last.

Sail on, Three Bells, forever,
    In grateful memory sail!
Ring on, Three Bells of rescue,
    Above the wave and gale!

Type of the Love eternal,
    Repeat the Master's cry,
As tossing through our darkness
    The lights of God draw nigh!

THE DEAD SHIP OF HARPSWELL

What flecks the outer gray beyond
    The sundown's golden trail?
The white flash of a sea-bird's wing,
    Or gleam of slanting sail?
Let young eyes watch from Neck and Point,
    And sea-worn elders pray,—
The ghost of what was once a ship
    Is sailing up the bay!

From gray sea-fog, from icy drift,
    From peril and from pain,
The home-bound fisher greets thy lights,
    O hundred-harbored Maine!
But many a keel shall seaward turn,
    And many a sail outstand,
When, tall and white, the Dead Ship looms
    Against the dusk of land.

She rounds the headland's bristling pines;
    She threads the isle-set bay;
No spur of breeze can speed her on,
    Nor ebb of tide delay.
Old men still walk the Isle of Orr
    Who tell her date and name,
Old shipwrights sit in Freeport yards
    Who hewed her oaken frame.

What weary doom of baffled quest,
    Thou sad sea-ghost, is thine?
What makes thee in the haunts of home
    A wonder and a sign?
No foot is on thy silent deck,
    Upon thy helm no hand;
No ripple hath the soundless wind
    That smites thee from the land!

For never comes the ship to port,
    Howe'er the breeze may be;
Just when she nears the waiting shore
    She drifts again to sea.
No tack of sail, nor turn of helm,
    Nor sheer of veering side;
Stern-fore she drives to sea and night,
    Against the wind and tide.

In vain o'er Harpswell Neck the star
    Of evening guides her in;

In vain for her the lamps are lit
    Within thy tower, Seguin!
In vain the harbor-boat shall hail,
    In vain the pilot call;
No hand shall reef her spectral sail,
    Or let her anchor fall.

Shake, brown old wives, with dreary joy,
    Your gray-head hints of ill;
And, over sick-beds whispering low,
    Your prophecies fulfill.
Some home amid yon birchen trees
    Shall drape its door with woe;
And slowly where the Dead Ship sails,
    The burial boat shall row!

From Wolf Neck and from Flying Point,
    From island and from main,
From sheltered cove and tided creek,
    Shall glide the funeral train.
The dead-boat with the bearers four,
    The mourners at her stern,—
And one shall go the silent way
    Who shall no more return!

And men shall sigh, and women weep,
    Whose dear ones pale and pine,
And sadly over sunset seas
    Await the ghostly sign.
They know not that its sails are filled
    By pity's tender breath,
Nor see the Angel at the helm
    Who steers the Ship of Death!

"Chill as a down-east breeze should be,"
    The Book-man said. "A ghostly touch
The legend has. I'm glad to see
    Your flying Yankee beat the Dutch."
"Well, here is something of the sort
    Which one midsummer day I caught
In Narragansett Bay, for lack of fish."
"We wait," the Traveller said; "serve hot or cold your dish."

SKIPPER IRESON'S RIDE

It is also claimed that the crew, rather than Skipper Ireson, refused to go to the aid of the sinking ship.

SKIPPER IRESON'S RIDE

Of all the rides since the birth of time,
Told in story or sung in rhyme,—
On Apuleius's Golden Ass,
Or one-eyed Calendar's horse of brass,
Witch astride of a human back,
Islam's prophet on Al-Borak,—
The strangest ride that ever was sped
Was Ireson's, out from Marblehead!
    Old Floyd Ireson, for his hard heart,
    Tarred and feathered and carried in a cart
        By the women of Marblehead!

Body of turkey, head of owl,
Wings a-droop like a rained-on fowl,
Feathered and ruffled in every part,
Skipper Ireson stood in the cart.
Scores of women, old and young,
Strong of muscle, and glib of tongue,
Pushed and pulled up the rocky lane,
Shouting and singing the shrill refrain:
    "Here's Flud Oirson, fur his horrd horrt,
    Torr'd an' futherr'd an' corr'd in a corrt
        By the women o' Morble'ead!"

Wrinkled scolds with hands on hips,
Girls in bloom of cheek and lips,
Wild-eyed, free-limbed, such as chase
Bacchus round some antique vase,
Brief of skirt, with ankles bare,
Loose of kerchief and loose of hair,
With conch-shells blowing and fish-horns twang,
Over and over the Mænads sang:
    "Here's Flud Oirson, fur his horrd horrt,
    Torr'd an' futherr'd an' corr'd in a corrt
        By the women o' Morble'ead!"

Small pity for him!—He sailed away
From a leaking ship, in Chaleur Bay,—
Sailed away from a sinking wreck,
With his own town's-people on her deck!
"Lay by! lay by!" they called to him.
Back he answered, "Sink or swim!
Brag of your catch of fish again!"
And off he sailed through the fog and rain!
    Old Floyd Ireson, for his hard heart,
    Tarred and feathered and carried in a cart
        By the women of Marblehead!

Fathoms deep in dark Chaleur
That wreck shall lie forevermore.
Mother and sister, wife and maid,
Looked from the rocks of Marblehead
Over the moaning and rainy sea,—
Looked for the coming that might not be!
What did the winds and the sea-birds say
Of the cruel captain who sailed away?—
   Old Floyd Ireson, for his hard heart,
   Tarred and feathered and carried in a cart
     By the women of Marblehead!

Through the street, on either side,
Up flew windows, doors swung wide;
Sharp-tongued spinsters, old wives gray,
Treble lent the fish-horn's bray.
Sea-worn grandsires, cripple-bound,
Hulks of old sailors run aground,
Shook head, and fist, and hat, and cane,
And cracked with curses the hoarse refrain:
   "Here's Flud Oirson, fur his horrd horrt,
   Torr'd an' futherr'd an' corr'd in a corrt
     By the women o' Morble'ead!"

Sweetly along the Salem road
Bloom of orchard and lilac showed.
Little the wicked skipper knew
Of the fields so green and the sky so blue,
Riding there in his sorry trim,
Like an Indian idol glum and grim,
Scarcely he seemed the sound to hear
Of voices shouting, far and near:
   "Here's Flud Oirson, fur his horrd horrt,
   Torr'd an' futherr'd an' corr'd in a corrt
     By the women o' Morble'ead!"

"Hear me, neighbors!" at last he cried,—
"What to me is this noisy ride?
What is the shame that clothes the skin
To the nameless horror that lives within?
Waking or sleeping, I see a wreck
And hear a cry from a reeling deck!
Hate me and curse me,—I only dread
The hand of God and the face of the dead!"
   Said old Floyd Ireson, for his hard heart,
   Tarred and feathered and carried in a cart
     By the women of Marblehead!

Then the wife of the skipper lost at sea
Said, "God has touched him,—why should we?"
Said an old wife mourning her only son,
"Cut the rogue's tether and let him run!"
So with soft relentings and rude excuse,
Half scorn, half pity, they cut him loose,
And gave him a cloak to hide him in,
And left him alone with his shame and sin.
   Poor Floyd Ireson, for his hard heart,
   Tarred and feathered and carried in a cart
     By the women of Marblehead!

THE SISTERS

Annie and Rhoda, sisters twain,
Woke in the night to the sound of rain,

The rush of wind, the ramp and roar
Of great waves climbing a rocky shore.

Annie rose up in her bed-gown white,
And looked out into the storm and night.

"Hush, and hearken!" she cried in fear,
"Hearest thou nothing, sister dear?"

"I hear the sea, and the plash of rain,
And roar of the northeast hurricane.

"Get thee back to the bed so warm,
No good comes of watching a storm.

"What is it to thee, I fain would know,
That waves are roaring and wild winds blow?

"No lover of thine's afloat to miss
The harbor-lights on a night like this."

"But I heard a voice cry out my name.
Up from the sea on the wind it came!

"Twice and thrice have I heard it call,
And the voice is the voice of Estwick Hall!"

On her pillow the sister tossed her head.
"Hall of the Heron is safe," she said.

"In the tautest schooner that ever swam
He rides at anchor in Anisquam.

"And, if in peril from swamping sea
Or lee shore rocks, would he call on thee?"

But the girl heard only the wind and tide,
And wringing her small white hands she cried:

"O sister Rhoda, there's something wrong;
I hear it again, so loud and long.

"'Annie; Annie!' I hear it call,
And the voice is the voice of Estwick Hall!"

Up sprang the elder, with eyes aflame;
"Thou liest! He never would call thy name!

"If he did, I would pray the wind and sea
To keep him forever from thee and me!"

Then out of the sea blew a dreadful blast;
Like the cry of a dying man it passed.

The young girl hushed on her lips a groan,
But through her tears a strange light shone,—

The solemn joy of her heart's release
To own and cherish its love in peace.

"Dearest!" she whispered, under breath,
"Life was a lie, but true is death.

"The love I hid from myself away
Shall crown me now in the light of day.

"My ears shall never to wooer list,
Never by lover my lips be kissed.

"Sacred to thee am I henceforth,
Thou in heaven and I on earth!"

She came and stood by her sister's bed;
"Hall of the Heron is dead!" she said.

"The wind and the waves their work have done,
We shall see him no more beneath the sun.

"Little will reck that heart of thine,
It loved him not with a love like mine.

"I, for his sake, were he but here,
Could hem and 'broider thy bridal gear,

"Though hands should tremble and eyes be wet,
And stitch for stitch in my heart be set.

"But now my soul with his soul I wed;
Thine the living, and mine the dead!"

THE WISHING BRIDGE

Among the legends sung or said
    Along our rocky shore,
The wishing Bridge of Marblehead
    May well be sung once more.

An hundred years ago (so ran
    The old-time story) all
Good wishes said above its span
    Would, soon or late, befall.

If pure and earnest, never failed
    The prayers of man or maid
For him who on the deep sea sailed,
    For her at home who stayed.

Once thither came two girls from school,
    And wished in childish glee;
And one would be a queen and rule,
    And one the world would see.

Time passed; with change of hopes and fears,
    And in the self-same place,
Two women, gray with middle years,
    Stood, wondering, face to face.

With wakened memories, as they met,
    They queried what had been:
"A poor man's wife am I, and yet,"
    Said one, "I am a queen.

"My realm a little homestead is,
    Where, lacking crown and throne,
I rule by loving services
    And patient toil alone."

The other said: "The great world lies
    Beyond me as it laid;
O'er love's and duty's boundaries
    My feet have never strayed.

"I see but common sights of home,
    Its common sounds I hear,
My widowed mother's sick-bed room
    Sufficeth for my sphere.

"I read to her some pleasant page
    Of travel far and wide,

And in a dreamy pilgrimage
  We wander side by side.

"And when, at last, she falls asleep,
  My book becomes to me
A magic glass: my watch I keep,
  But all the world I see.

"A farm-wife queen your place you fill,
  While fancy's privilege
Is mine to walk the earth at will,
  Thanks to the Wishing Bridge."

"Nay, leave the legend for the truth,"
  The other cried, "and say
God gives the wishes of our youth
  But in His own best way!"

THE BAY OF SEVEN ISLANDS

The skipper sailed out of the harbor mouth,
Leaving the apple-bloom of the South
  For the ice of the Eastern seas,
  In his fishing schooner Breeze.

Handsome and brave and young was he,
And the maids of Newbury sighed to see
  His lessening white sail fall
  Under the sea's blue wall.

Through the Northern Gulf and the misty screen
Of the isles of Mingan and Madeleine,
  St. Paul's and Blanc Sablon,
  The little Breeze sailed on,

Backward and forward, along the shore
Of lorn and desolate Labrador,
  And found at last her way
  To the Seven Islands Bay.

The little hamlet, nestling below
Great hills white with lingering snow,
  With its tin-roofed chapel stood
  Half hid in the dwarf spruce wood;

Green-turfed, flower-sown, the last outpost
Of summer upon the dreary coast,
  With its gardens small and spare,
  Sad in the frosty air.

THE BAY OF SEVEN ISLANDS

Hard by where the skipper's schooner lay,
A fisherman's cottage looked away
    Over isle and bay, and behind
    On mountains dim-defined.

And there twin sisters, fair and young,
Laughed with their stranger guest, and sung
    In their native tongue the lays
    Of the old Provencal days.

Alike were they, save the faint outline
Of a scar on Suzette's forehead fine;
    And both, it so befell,
    Loved the heretic stranger well.

Both were pleasant to look upon,
But the heart of the skipper clave to one;
    Though less by his eye than heart
    He knew the twain apart.

Despite of alien race and creed,
Well did his wooing of Marguerite speed;
    And the mother's wrath was vain
    As the sister's jealous pain.

The shrill-tongued mistress her house forbade,
And solemn warning was sternly said
    By the black-robed priest, whose word
    As law the hamlet heard.

But half by voice and half by signs
The skipper said, "A warm sun shines
    On the green-banked Merrimac;
    Wait, watch, till I come back.

"And when you see, from my mast head,
The signal fly of a kerchief red,
    My boat on the shore shall wait;
    Come, when the night is late."

Ah, weighed with childhood's haunts and friends,
And all that the home sky overbends,
    Did ever young love fail
    To turn the trembling scale?

Under the night, on the wet sea sands
Slowly unclasped their plighted hands:
    One to the cottage hearth,
    And one to his sailor's berth.

What was it the parting lovers heard?
Nor leaf, nor ripple, nor wing of bird,
    But a listener's stealthy tread
    On the rock-moss, crisp and dead.

He weighed his anchor, and fished once more
By the black coast-line of Labrador;
    And by love and the north wind driven,
    Sailed back to the Islands Seven.

In the sunset's glow the sisters twain
Saw the Breeze come sailing in again;
    Said Suzette, "Mother dear,
    The heretic's sail is here."

"Go, Marguerite, to your room, and hide;
Your door shall be bolted!" the mother cried:
    While Suzette, ill at ease,
    Watched the red sign of the Breeze.

At midnight, down to the waiting skiff
She stole in the shadow of the cliff;
    And out of the Bay's mouth ran
    The schooner with maid and man.

And all night long, on a restless bed,
Her prayers to the Virgin Marguerite said;
    And thought of her lover's pain
    Waiting for her in vain.

Did he pace the sands? Did he pause to hear
The sound of her light step drawing near?
    And, as the slow hours passed,
    Would he doubt her faith at last?

But when she saw through the misty pane,
The morning break on a sea of rain,
    Could even her love avail
    To follow his vanished sail?

Meantime the Breeze, with favoring wind,
Left the rugged Moisic hills behind,
    And heard from an unseen shore
    The falls of Manitou roar.

On the morrow's morn, in the thick gray weather
They sat on the reeling deck together,
    Lover and counterfeit,
    Of hapless Marguerite.

With a lover's hand, from her forehead fair
He smoothed away her jet-black hair.
    What was it his fond eyes met?
    The scar of the false Suzette!

Fiercely he shouted: "Bear away
East by north for Seven Isles Bay!"
    The maiden wept and prayed,
    But the ship her helm obeyed.

Once more the Bay of the Isles they found:
They heard the bell of the chapel sound,
    And the chant of the dying sung
    In the harsh, wild Indian tongue.

A feeling of mystery, change, and awe
Was in all they heard and all they saw:
    Spell-bound the hamlet lay
    In the hush of its lonely bay.

And when they came to the cottage door,
The mother rose up from her weeping sore,
    And with angry gestures met
    The scared look of Suzette.

"Here is your daughter," the skipper said;
"Give me the one I love instead."
    But the woman sternly spake;
    "Go, see if the dead will wake!"

He looked. Her sweet face still and white
And strange in the noonday taper light,
    She lay on her little bed,
    With the cross at her feet and head.

In a passion of grief the strong man bent
Down to her face, and, kissing it, went
    Back to the waiting Breeze,
    Back to the mournful seas.

Never again to the Merrimac
And Newbury's homes that bark came back.
    Whether her fate she met
    On the shores of Carraquette,

Miscou, or Tracadie, who can say?
But even yet at Seven Isles Bay
    Is told the ghostly tale
    Of a weird, unspoken sail,

In the pale, sad light of the Northern day
Seen by the blanketed Montagnais,
    Or squaw, in her small kyack,
    Crossing the spectre's track.

On the deck a maiden wrings her hands;
Her likeness kneels on the gray coast sands;
    One in her wild despair,
    And one in the trance of prayer.

She flits before no earthly blast,
The red sign fluttering from her mast,
    Over the solemn seas,
    The ghost of the schooner Breeze!

THE SISTERS
A Picture by Barry

The shade for me, but over thee
    The lingering sunshine still;
As, smiling, to the silent stream
    Comes down the singing rill.

So come to me, my little one,—
    My years with thee I share,
And mingle with a sister's love
    A mother's tender care.

But keep the smile upon thy lip,
    The trust upon thy brow;
Since for the dear one God hath called
    We have an angel now.

Our mother from the fields of heaven
    Shall still her ear incline;
Nor need we fear her human love
    Is less for love divine.

The songs are sweet they sing beneath
    The trees of life so fair,
But sweetest of the songs of heaven
    Shall be her children's prayer.

Then, darling, rest upon my breast,
    And teach my heart to lean
With thy sweet trust upon the arm
    Which folds us both unseen!

THE TWO ANGELS

God called the nearest angels who dwell with Him above:
The tenderest one was Pity, the dearest one was Love.

"Arise " He said, "my angels! a wail of woe and sin
Steals through the gates of heaven, and saddens all within.

"My harps take up the mournful strain that from a lost world swells,
The smoke of torment clouds the light and blights the asphodels.

"Fly downward to that under world, and on its souls of pain
Let Love drop smiles like sunshine, and Pity tears like rain!"

Two faces bowed before the Throne, veiled in their golden hair;
Four white wings lessened swiftly down the dark abyss of air.

The way was strange, the flight was long; at last the angels came
Where swung the lost and nether world, red-wrapped in rayless flame.

There Pity, shuddering, wept; but Love, with faith too strong for fear,
Took heart from God's almightiness and smiled a smile of cheer.

And lo! that tear of Pity quenched the flame whereon it fell,
And, with the sunshine of that smile, hope entered into hell!

Two unveiled faces full of joy looked upward to the Throne,
Four white wings folded at the feet of Him who sat thereon!

And deeper than the sound of seas, more soft than falling flake,
Amidst the hush of wing and song the Voice Eternal spake:

"Welcome, my angels! ye have brought a holier joy to heaven;
Henceforth its sweetest song shall be the song of sin forgiven!"

GIVING AND TAKING

Whittier put in English verse a prose translation of a poem by Tinnevaluva, a Hindoo poet of the third century.

Who gives and hides the giving hand,
   Nor counts on favor, fame, or praise,
   Shall find his smallest gift outweighs
The burden of the sea and land.

Who gives to whom hath naught been given,
    His gift in need, though small indeed
    As is the grass-blade's wind-blown seed,
Is large as earth and rich as heaven.

Forget it not, O man, to whom
    A gift shall fall, while yet on earth;
    Yea, even to thy seven-fold birth
Recall it in the lives to come.

Who broods above a wrong in thought
    Sins much; but greater sin is his
    Who, fed and clothed with kindnesses,
Shall count the holy alms as nought.

Who dares to curse the hands that bless
    Shall know of sin the deadliest cost;
    The patience of the heavens is lost
Beholding man's unthankfulness.

For he who breaks all laws may still
    In Sivam's mercy be forgiven;
    But none can save, in earth or heaven,
The wretch who answers good with ill.

A WOMAN

O, dwarfed and wronged, and stained with ill,
Behold! thou art a woman still!
And, by that sacred name and dear,
I bid thy better self appear.
Still, through thy foul disguise, I see
The rudimental purity,
That, spite of change and loss, makes good
Thy birthright-claim of womanhood;
An inward loathing, deep, intense;
A shame that is half innocence.
Cast off the grave-clothes of thy sin!
Rise from the dust thou liest in,
As Mary rose at Jesus' word,
Redeemed and white before the Lord!
Reclaim thy lost soul! In His name,
Rise up, and break thy bonds of shame.
Art weak? He's strong, Art fearful! Hear
The world's O'ercomer: "Be of cheer!"
What lip shall judge when He approves?
Who dare to scorn the child he loves?

THE WATCHERS

Beside a stricken field I stood;
On the torn turf, on grass and wood
Hung heavily the dew of blood.

Still in their fresh mounds lay the slain,
But all the air was quick with pain
And gusty sighs and tearful rain.

Two angels, each with drooping head
And folded wings and noiseless tread,
Watched by that valley of the dead.

The one, with forehead saintly bland
And lips of blessing, not command,
Leaned, weeping, on her olive wand.

The other's brows were scarred and knit,
His restless eyes were watch-fires lit,
His hands for battle-gauntlets fit.

"How long!"—I knew the voice of Peace,—
"Is there no respite?—no release?—
When shall the hopeless quarrel cease?

"O Lord, how long!—One human soul
Is more than any parchment scroll,
Or any flag thy winds unroll.

"What price was Ellsworth's, young and brave?
How weigh the gift that Lyon gave,
Or count the cost of Winthrop's grave?

"O brother! if thine eye can see,
Tell how and when the end shall be,
What hope remains for thee and me."

Then Freedom sternly said: "I shun
No strife nor pang beneath the sun,
When human rights are staked and won.

"I knelt with Ziska's hunted flock,
I watched in Toussaint's cell of rock,
I walked with Sidney to the block.

"The moor of Marston felt my tread,
Through Jersey snows the march I led,
My voice Magenta's charges sped.

"But now, through weary day and night,
I watch a vague and aimless fight
For leave to strike one blow aright.

"On either side my foe they own:
One guards through love his ghastly throne,
And one through fear to reverence grown.

"Why wait we longer, mocked, betrayed,
By open foes, or those afraid
To speed thy coming through my aid?

"Why watch to see who win or fall?—
I shake the dust against them all,
I leave them to their senseless brawl."

"Nay," Peace implored: "yet longer wait;
The doom is near, the stake is great:
God knoweth if it be too late.

"Still wait and watch; the way prepare
Where I with folded wings of prayer
May follow, weaponless and bare."

"Too late!" the stern, sad voice replied,
"Too late!" its mournful echo sighed,
In low lament the answer died.

A rustling as of wings in flight,
An upward gleam of lessening white,
So passed the vision, sound and sight.

But round me, like a silver bell
Rung down the listening sky to tell
Of holy help, a sweet voice fell.

"Still hope and trust," it sang; "the rod
Must fall, the wine-press must be trod,
But all is possible with God!"

SAINT GREGORY'S GUEST

A tale for Roman guides to tell
    To careless, sight-worn travellers still,
Who pause beside the narrow cell
    Of Gregory on the Cælian Hill.

One day before the monk's door came
    A beggar, stretching empty palms,
Fainting and fast-sick, in the name
    Of the Most Holy asking alms.

SAINT GREGORY'S GUEST

And the monk answered, "All I have
    In this poor cell of mine I give,
The silver cup my mother gave;
    In Christ's name take thou it, and live."

Years passed; and, called at last to bear
    Pastoral crook and keys of Rome
The poor monk, in Saint Peter's chair,
    Sat the crowned lord of Christendom.

"Prepare a feast," Saint Gregory cried,
    "And let twelve beggars sit thereat."
The beggars came, and one beside,
    An unknown stranger, with them sat.

"I asked thee not," the Pontiff spake,
    "O stranger; but if need be thine,
I bid thee welcome, for the sake
    Of Him who is thy Lord and mine."

A grave, calm face the stranger raised,
    Like His who on Gennesaret trod,
Or His on whom the Chaldeans gazed,
    Whose form was as the Son of God.

"Know'st thou," he said, "thy gift of old?"
    And in the hand he lifted up
The Pontiff marvelled to behold
    Once more his mother's silver cup.

"Thy prayers and alms have risen, and bloom
    Sweetly among the flowers of heaven.
I am The Wonderful, through whom
    Whate'er thou askest shall be given."

He spake and vanished. Gregory fell
    With his twelve guests in mute accord
Prone on their faces, knowing well
    Their eyes of flesh had seen the Lord.

The old-time legend is not vain;
    Nor vain thy art, Verona's Paul,
Telling it o'er and o'er again
    On gray Vicenza's frescoed wall.

Still wheresoever pity shares
    Its bread with sorrow, want, and sin,
And love the beggar's feast prepares,
    The uninvited Guest comes in.

Unheard, because our ears are dull,
    Unseen, because our eyes are dim,
He walks our earth, The Wonderful,
    And all good deeds are done to Him.

THE REWARD

Who, looking backward from his manhood's prime,
Sees not the spectre of his misspent time?
    And through the shade
Of funeral cypress planted thick behind,
Hears no reproachful whisper on the wind
    From his loved dead?

Who bears no trace of passion's evil force?
Who shuns thy sting, O terrible Remorse?—
    Who does not cast
On the thronged pages of his memory's book,
At times, a sad and half-reluctant look,
    Regretful of the past?

Alas!—the evil which we fain would shun
We do, and leave the wished-for good undone:
    Our strength today
Is but tomorrow's weakness, prone to fall;
Poor, blind, unprofitable servants all
    Are we alway.

Yet who, thus looking backward o'er his years,
Feels not his eyelids wet with grateful tears,
    If he hath been
Permitted, weak and sinful as he was
To cheer and aid, in some ennobling cause,
    His fellow-men?

If he hath hidden the outcast, or let in
A ray of sunshine to the cell of sin,—
    If he hath lent
Strength to the weak, and, in an hour of need,
Over the suffering, mindless of his creed
    Or home, hath bent,

He has not lived in vain, and while he gives
The praise to Him, in whom he moves and lives,
    With thankful heart;
He gazes backward, and with hope before,
Knowing that from his works he nevermore
    Can henceforth part.

THE ETERNAL GOODNESS

O friends! with whom my feet have trod
    The quiet aisles of prayer,
Glad witness to your zeal for God
    And love of man I bear.

I trace your lines of argument;
    Your logic linked and strong
I weigh as one who dreads dissent,
    And fears a doubt as wrong.

But still my human hands are weak
    To hold your iron creeds:
Against the words ye bid me speak
    My heart within me pleads.

Who fathoms the Eternal Thought?
    Who talks of scheme and plan?
The Lord is God! He needeth not
    The poor device of man.

I walk with bare, hushed feet the ground
    Ye tread with boldness shod;
I dare not fix with mete and bound
    The love and power of God.

Ye praise His justice; even such
    His pitying love I deem:
Ye seek a king; I fain would touch
    The robe that hath no seam.

Ye see the curse which overbroods
    A world of pain and loss;
I hear our Lord's beatitudes
    And prayer upon the cross.

More than your schoolmen teach, within
    Myself, alas! I know:
Too dark ye cannot paint the sin,
    Too small the merit show.

I bow my forehead to the dust,
    I veil mine eyes for shame,
And urge, in trembling self-distrust,
    A prayer without a claim.

I see the wrong that round me lies,
    I feel the guilt within;
I hear, with groan and travail-cries,
    The word confess its sin.

THE ETERNAL GOODNESS

Yet, in the maddening maze of things,
    And tossed by storm and flood,
To one fixed trust my spirit clings;
    I know that God is good!

Not mine to look where cherubim
    And seraphs may not see,
But nothing can be good in Him
    Which evil is in me.

The wrong that pains my soul below
    I dare not throne above:
I know not of His hate,—I know
    His goodness and His love.

I dimly guess from blessings known
    Of greater out of sight,
And, with the chastened Psalmist, own
    His judgments too are right.

I long for household voices gone,
    For vanished smiles I long,
But God hath led my dear ones on,
    And He can do no wrong.

I know not what the future hath
    Of marvel or surprise,
Assured alone that life and death
    His mercy underlies.

And if my heart and flesh are weak
    To bear an untried pain,
The bruised reed He will not break,
    But strengthen and sustain.

No offering of my own I have,
    Nor works my faith to prove;
I can but give the gifts He gave,
    And plead His love for love.

And so beside the Silent Sea
    I wait the muffled oar;
No harm from Him can come to me
    On ocean or on shore.

I know not where His islands lift
    Their fronded palms in air;
I only know I cannot drift
    Beyond His love and care.

O brothers! if my faith is vain,
   If hopes like these betray,
Pray for me that my feet may gain
   The sure and safer way.

And Thou, O Lord! by whom are seen
   Thy creatures as they be,
Forgive me if too close I lean
   My human heart on Thee!

THY WILL BE DONE

We see not, know not; all our way
Is night,—with Thee alone is day.
From out the torrent's troubled drift,
Above the storm our prayers we lift,
   Thy will be done!

The flesh may fail, the heart may faint,
But who are we to make complaint,
Or dare to plead, in times like these,
The weakness of our love of ease?
   Thy will be done!

We take with solemn thankfulness
Our burden up, nor ask it less,
And count it joy that even we
May suffer, serve, or wait for Thee,
   Whose will be done!

Though dim as yet in tint and line,
We trace Thy picture's wise design,
And thank Thee that our age supplies
Its dark relief of sacrifice.
   Thy will be done!

And if, in our unworthiness,
Thy sacrificial wine we press;
If from Thy ordeal's heated bars
Our feet are seamed with crimson scars,
   Thy will be done!

If, for the age to come, this hour
Of trial hath vicarious power,
And, blest by Thee, our present pain,
Be Liberty's eternal gain,
   Thy will be done!

Strike, Thou the Master, we Thy keys,
The anthem of the destinies!
The minor of Thy loftier strain,
Our hearts shall breathe the old refrain,
    Thy will be done!

THE WISH OF TODAY

I ask not now for gold to gild
    With mocking shine a weary frame;
The yearning of the mind is stilled,—
    I ask not now for Fame.

A rose-cloud, dimly seen above,
    Melting in heaven's blue depths away,—
O, sweet, fond dream of human Love!
    For thee I may not pray.

But, bowed in lowliness of mind,
    I make my humble wishes known,—
I only ask a will resigned,
    O Father, to thine own!

Today, beneath thy chastening eye
    I crave alone for peace and rest,
Submissive in thy hand to lie,
    And feel that it is best.

A marvel seems the Universe,
    A miracle our Life and Death;
A mystery which I cannot pierce,
    Around, above, beneath.

In vain I task my aching brain,
    In vain the sage's thought I scan,
I only feel how weak and vain,
    How poor and blind, is man.

And now my spirit sighs for home,
    And longs for light whereby to see,
And, like a weary child, would come,
    O Father, unto thee!

Though oft, like letters traced on sand,
    My weak resolves have passed away,
In mercy lend thy helping hand
    Unto my prayer to-day!

AT LAST

When on my day of life the night is falling,
    And, in the winds from unsunned spaces blown,
I hear far voices out of darkness calling
    My feet to paths unknown,

Thou who hast made my home of life so pleasant,
    Leave not its tenant when its walls decay;
O Love Divine, O Helper ever present,
    Be Thou my strength and stay!

Be near me when all else is from me drifting:
    Earth, sky, home's pictures, days of shade and shine,
And kindly faces to my own uplifting
    The love which answers mine.

I have but Thee, my Father! let Thy spirit
    Be with me then to comfort and uphold;
No gate of pearl, no branch of palm I merit,
    Nor street of shining gold.

Suffice it if—my good and ill unreckoned,
    And both forgiven through Thy abounding grace—
I find myself by hands familiar beckoned
    Unto my fitting place.

Some humble door among Thy many mansions,
    Some sheltering shade where sin and striving cease,
And flows forever through heaven's green expansions
    The river of Thy peace.

There, from the music round about me stealing,
    I fain would learn the new and holy song,
And find at last, beneath Thy trees of healing,
    The life for which I long.

HAVERHILL

1640-1890

Read at the Celebration of the Two Hundred and Fiftieth Anniversary of the City, July 2, 1890.

O RIVER winding to the sea!
We call the old time back to thee;
From forest paths and water-ways
The century-woven veil we raise.

The voices of to-day are dumb,
Unheard its sounds that go and come;
We listen, through long-lapsing years,
To footsteps of the pioneers.

Gone steepled town and cultured plain,
The wilderness returns again,
The drear, untrodden solitude,
The gloom and mystery of the wood!

Once more the bear and panther prowl,
The wolf repeats his hungry howl,
And, peering through his leafy screen,
The Indian's copper face is seen.

We see, their rude-built huts beside,
Grave men and women anxious-eyed,
And wistful youth remembering still
Dear homes in England's Haverhill.

We summon forth to mortal view
Dark Passaquo and Saggahew,—
Wild chiefs, who owned the mighty sway
Of wizard Passaconaway.

Weird memories of the border town,
By old tradition handed down,
In chance and change before us pass
Like pictures in a magic glass,—

The terror of the midnight raid,
The death-concealing ambuscade,
The winter march, through deserts wild,
Of captive mother, wife, and child.

Ah! bleeding hands alone subdued
And tamed the savage habitude
Of forests hiding beasts of prey,
And human shapes as fierce as they.

Slow from the plough the woods withdrew,
Slowly each year the corn-lands grew;
Nor fire, nor frost, nor foe could kill
The Saxon energy of will.

And never in the hamlet's bound
Was lack of sturdy manhood found,
And never failed the kindred good
Of brave and helpful womanhood.

That hamlet now a city is,
Its log-built huts are palaces;
The wood-path of the settler's cow
Is Traffic's crowded highway now.

And far and wide it stretches still,
Along its southward sloping hill,
And overlooks on either hand
A rich and many-watered land.

And, gladdening all the landscape, fair
As Pison was to Eden's pair,
Our river to its valley brings
The blessing of its mountain springs.

And Nature holds with narrowing space,
From mart and crowd, her old-time grace,
And guards with fondly jealous arms
The wild growths of outlying farms.

Her sunsets of Kenoza fall,
Her autumn leaves by Saltonstall;
No lavished gold can richer make
Her opulence of hill and lake.

Wise was the choice which led our sires
To kindle here their household fires,
And share the large content of all
Whose lines in pleasant places fall.

More dear, as years on years advance,
We prize the old inheritance,
And feel, as far and wide we roam,
That all we seek we leave at home.

Our palms are pines, our oranges
Are apples on our orchard trees;
Our thrushes are our nightingales,
Our larks the blackbirds of our vales.

No incense which the Orient burns
Is sweeter than our hillside ferns;
What tropic splendor can outvie
Our autumn woods, our sunset sky?

If, where the slow years came and went,
And left not affluence, but content,
Now flashes in our dazzled eyes
The electric light of enterprise;

And if the old idyllic ease
Seems lost in keen activities,
And crowded workshops now replace
The hearth's and farm-field's rustic grace;

No dull, mechanic round of toil
Life's morning charm can quite despoil;
And youth and beauty, hand in hand,
Will always find enchanted land.

No task is ill where hand and brain
And skill and strength have equal gain,
And each shall each in honor hold,
And simple manhood outweigh gold.

Earth shall be near to Heaven when all
That severs man from man shall fall,
For, here or there, salvation's plan
Alone is love of God and man.

O dwellers by the Merrimac,
The heirs of centuries at your back,
Still reaping where you have not sown,
A broader field is now your own.

Hold fast your Puritan heritage,
But let the free thought of the age
Its light and hope and sweetness add
To the stern faith the fathers had.

Adrift on Time's returnless tide,
As waves that follow waves, we glide.
God grant we leave upon the shore
Some waif of good it lacked before;

Some seed, or flower, or plant of worth,
Some added beauty to the earth;
Some larger hope, some thought to make
The sad world happier for its sake.

As tenants of uncertain stay,
So may we live our little day
That only grateful hearts shall fill
The homes we leave in Haverhill.

The singer of a farewell rhyme,
Upon whose outmost verge of time
The shades of nights are falling down,
I pray, God bless the good old town!

INDEX TO POEMS

At Last	139
Barbara Frietchie	30
Barefoot Boy	32
Bay of Seven Islands	124
Captain's Well	83
Cassandra Southwick	89
Christian Slave	52
Corn Song	80
Countess	40
Dead Ship of Harpswell	117
Eternal Goodness	135
Exile's Departure	13
Farewell of Virginia Slave Mother	53
Giving and Taking	129
Haverhill	140
How the Women Went from Dover	94
Huskers	79
Ichabod	64
Kansas Emigrant	65
Kathleen	86
King's Missive	105
Marguerite	97
Massachusetts to Virginia	56
Maud Muller	34
Memories	37
Merrimack	71
Molock in State Street	59
New Wife and the Old	112

Our State	45
Pentucket 1708	69
Poor Voter on Election Day	68
Prisoner for Debt	66
Reward	134
Sabbath Scene	61
Saint Gregory's Guest	132
School Days	39
Shoemakers	77
Sisters	121
Sisters – a Picture	128
Skipper Ireson's Ride	118
Slave Ships	48
Snow Bound	14
Stanzas	45
Sycamores	73
Telling the Bees	82
Three Bells	116
Thy Will Be Done	137
Two Angels	129
Watchers	131
Wishing Bridge	123
Wish of Today	138
Witch of Wenham	99
Woman	130
Wreck at Rivermouth	108
Yankee Girl	55